THE
REHNQUIST COURT

**Recent Titles in
Contributions in Legal Studies**

The Politics of Obscenity: Group Litigation in a Time of Legal Change
Joseph F. Kobylka

An Essential Safeguard: Essays on the United States Supreme Court
and Its Justices
D. Grier Stephenson, Jr., editor

A "Representative" Supreme Court? The Impact of Race, Religion, and
Gender on Appointments
Barbara A. Perry

State Constitutions and Criminal Justice
Barry Latzer

The Sixth Amendment in Modern American Jurisprudence:
A Critical Perspective
Alfredo Garcia

Positive Neutrality: Letting Religious Freedom Ring
Stephen V. Monsma

Questioning the Law in Corporate America: Agenda for Reform
Gerald L. Houseman

Reason Over Precedents: Origins of American Legal Thought
Craig Evan Klafter

The Iron Horse and the Constitution: The Railroads and the
Transformation of the Fourteenth Amendment
Richard C. Cortner

Between Civil and Religious Law: The Flight of the *Agunah* in
American Society
Irving A. Breitowitz

The Death Penalty and Racial Bias: Overturning Supreme Court
Assumptions
Gregory D. Russel

THE
REHNQUIST COURT

In Pursuit of Judicial Conservatism

STANLEY H. FRIEDELBAUM

Contributions in Legal Studies, Number 76
PAUL L. MURPHY, SERIES EDITOR

Greenwood Press
Westport, Connecticut • London

Library of Congress Cataloging-in-Publication Data

Friedelbaum, Stanley H. (Stanley Herman).
    The Rehnquist court : in pursuit of judicial conservatism /
Stanley H. Friedelbaum.
        p. cm.—(Contributions in legal studies, ISSN 0147–1074 ;
no. 76)
    Includes bibliographical references and index.
    ISBN 0–313–27990–X (alk. paper)
    1. United States. Supreme Court. 2. Political questions and
judicial power—United States. 3. Conservatism—United States.
I. Title. II. Series.
KF8748.F78   1994
347. 73'26—dc20
[347.30735]   93–14122

British Library Cataloguing in Publication Data is available.

Library of Congress Catalog Card Number: 93–14122
ISBN: 0–313–27990–X
ISSN: 0147–1074

First published in 1994

Greenwood Press, 88 Post Road West, Westport, CT 06881
An imprint of Greenwood Publishing Group, Inc.

Printed in the United States of America

The paper used in this book complies with the
Permanent Paper Standard issued by the National
Information Standards Organization (Z39.48–1984).

10 9 8 7 6 5 4 3 2

To Claire
Whose love of literature and books helped more than she
could have realized

and

To Barbara
whose devotion to the law and its practice has taken on
new and far more personal attributes.

Contents

Preface

The preparation of a study analyzing the work of the U.S Supreme Court gives rise to a challenging, if not a daunting effort. In a book of modest length, it is futile to attempt even a brief review of all salient phases of the Rehnquist Court's offerings. Selectivity serves as the guiding principle both for the observer and for the Justices though, it must be conceded, topical choices do betray an attraction to or an aversion to certain subjects drawn from the judicial universe. Over more than two centuries since the founding of the Republic, the Court has always been an institution reviewing a variety of issues but still committed, at least minimally, to the preservation of historic ideals that transcend ephemeral concerns. It is from a vast array that the Justices must choose in deciding which cases merit plenary consideration. In like fashion, but fortunately with fewer social or political ramifications, an observer is required to select among the diverse subject-areas to which the Court's attention has been directed.

Choices doubtless reflect value judgments regarding the most significant areas, and whether and how each ought to be explored. But themes and interests have changed markedly in little more than two decades. If a broad range of topics may be designated for critical analysis, the contemporary Court reveals substantial differences from its predecessors, even those of recent date. The Warren Court, long recognized as an avant-garde tribunal, never ventured upon consideration of such currently debated issues as the reach of personal autonomy generally defined, right-to-die procedures in particular, the existence of a constitutionally sanctioned right of abortion, the validity of sundry restrictive statutes and regulations, privacy interests and substantive due process, and affirmative action and reverse discrimination. In this light, the Rehnquist Court has weighed controversial policy questions formerly taken to be beyond the ken of judicial inquiry and resolution. The Warren Court declined to consider these issues encumbered, as it was, by disputes over justiciability, contention during the final stages of the "nationalization" of the Bill of Rights, and disagreement relating to the breadth of guarantees found within more conventional constitutional settings. Thus the judicial horizon is notably unlike its antecedents even as long-term problems, such as those associated with federalism and the separation of powers, recur and provide limited elements of continuity.

Questions may reasonably be raised respecting the appropriateness of a work on the Rehnquist Court at a time when a new administration in Washington promises to bring about important changes in judicial personnel. That the Court's prevailing majority will continue to govern for some years appears virtually assured as a result of the relative "youthfulness" of the Reagan-Bush appointees. More to the point perhaps is the recent emergence of a new centrist coalition that may control in cases touching upon critical subject-matter areas. Yet an essentially conservative Rehnquist Court is not likely to change course dramatically even if the new coalition holds and imparts a sense of moderation to judicial deliberations and to some of the resulting opinions. All that may be expected in a study of the Court's decisional output is a balanced, albeit critical, account of its most significant activities, embodying both advances and reverses, free of polemics and prejudgments based upon past performance and associations.

Interest in undertaking this study was prompted by my participation in a work providing biographical sketches and analytical
reviews of the Burger Court Justices. The results, as the book's title
suggests, were centered about the several judicial actors concerned,
though case critiques necessarily pertained to the major areas of
constitutional law.[1] It occurred to me that a study of the Rehnquist
Court as a functional unit would provide a useful contribution and
would offer points of departure for students of judicial politics and
of contemporary doctrinal developments. Few doubt that the Supreme Court will continue to exercise responsible leadership even
as judicial federalism grows apace and state appellate courts reassume their rightful status as co-participants in the crafting of
American constitutionalism. An account of the work of the
Rehnquist Court, no less than one assessing the products of the
Burger years, surely is in order.

A number of the case analyses represented in this volume were
first undertaken in my presentations to graduate classes and honors
seminars. I am grateful for the intellectual stimulation provided by
those participating. My thanks extend to the staffs of the several
libraries in the Rutgers multi-campus system, especially in facilitating access to advance sheets that provided new perspectives
drawn from opinions of the trial and intermediate-level federal
courts and of the state courts. For a careful and thoughtful typing
of the manuscript in its several stages, I most appreciate the able
secretarial assistance of Maryann Borko Privrat. Mildred Vasan of
Greenwood Press offered support from the outset and expressed
confidence in this project when it was most needed.

NOTE

1. THE BURGER COURT: POLITICAL AND JUDICIAL PROFILES (Charles M. Lamb
and Stephen C. Halpern, eds., 1991).

Introduction

With the departure of Justice William Brennan from the Supreme Court during the summer of 1990, a new era—one that was inaugurated at least half a decade earlier—has taken on an aura of reality and has displayed distinctive attributes that may extend into the coming century. It is always difficult and often perilous to attempt to characterize a court by reference to a change in the presiding chief justice. Yet President Ronald Reagan's elevation of William Rehnquist to the post in 1986 marked a turning point in the Court's decisional outlook accompanied, as it was soon to be, by the appointments of Antonin Scalia and Anthony Kennedy as associate justices. President George Bush's subsequent nomination of David Souter to replace Justice Brennan promised to solidify the new voting bloc if, in fact, this was necessary in light of Justice Byron White's increasingly close association with the views expressed by the prevailing majority. More recently, with the retirement of Justice Thurgood Marshall, another acknowledged conservative, Clarence Thomas, joined the Court following a wrenching confirmation debate in the Senate. The Rehnquist Court, then, has come to represent a working coalition of six or seven members who, more often than not, share common public policy goals.

All the same, it should not be assumed that anything akin to a solid voting bloc categorically describes this or any other court. Consensus among the Justices may best be depicted as an affinity linked to subject-matter, defined narrowly and specifically. Within its limits, the assignment of political labels, such as liberal and conservative, may be useful. Yet at times the Justices will and have departed from their assigned roles and claimed political attachments—so much so as to cause consternation among court-watchers. Few could have predicted, with any degree of accuracy, that Justices Scalia and Kennedy would join Justice Brennan and the liberal faction in sustaining First Amendment rights in the flag-burning cases.[1] The dissenters on both occasions consisted of Chief Justice Rehnquist and Justices O'Connor, White, and Stevens. The latter, long regarded as a judicial maverick, joined this unaccustomed coalition because of his conviction that any affront to freedom of expression was trivial and that the symbolic value of the flag as a national asset outweighed any First Amendment incursions. If the flag desecration cases strike the observer as atypical and conceived in a highly charged atmosphere, less dramatic departures from well-trodden paths also have arisen in more mundane contexts.

The Rehnquist Court reflects a legacy combining, in part, the avant-garde rulings of the Warren years and those of the less activist-oriented Burger Court. Despite fears of a widespread repudiation of Warren Court precedents in the 1970s, the Burger Court moved with care in reviewing and in modifying previous holdings. Any significant retreat, when it occurred, came slowly and was usually confined to marginal alterations. Backsliding was limited to aspects of the criminal law while, in some areas, innovations were introduced into the decisional calculus. The Court was often looked upon as a transitional one. In fact, thematic advances in cases touching upon privacy rights generally and heterosexual relations and personal autonomy[2] in particular were in evidence. Significant indicators of continuity, spanning both the Warren and Burger years, were also discernible.

The Burger Court's return to a jurisprudence of moderation and, at times, even of diffidence in regard to a variety of issues has reappeared in a number of decisions marking the early years of the Rehnquist Court. More than half a century has passed since the Court announced a broad doctrine of deference touching upon aspects of economic and social legislation, whether passed by Congress or by the state legislatures. Adherence to the doctrine, with periodic reaffirmations of a familiar litany sustaining fidelity to it, has not been seriously questioned.

A notably limited revival of substantive due process, long an object of judicial disdain, served as the basis for the selective creation of rights of individual personal autonomy and for safeguarding the sanctity of conjugal relations during the Burger years. While the Rehnquist Court has not abandoned the precedents established, there has been a tendency, especially with respect to abortion rights, to diminish markedly the effectiveness and breadth of these rulings. The Rehnquist majority has shown a distinct disinclination to expand the concept of due process liberty that, in the Burger Court, had contributed to a "new" bill of rights instituted by judicial fiat.[3] Yet the Court upheld a liberty interest in the first right-to-die case that, somewhat surprisingly, it agreed to review.[4] On balance, caution, an aversion to embark upon novel ventures in decision making, and dismayingly regressive exploits mark the Rehnquist Court, although its activities ought hardly to be characterized as a major withdrawal from judgment.

Interestingly, affirmative action and civil rights cases have revealed a partial countertrend, that is, the tendency of the Court to preserve basically unsullied the essential elements of prior decisional law though with more than peripheral changes appended to them. The Court's performance in advancing the sweep of "benignity" in a group rights perspective[5] minimally outweighed earlier thrusts rejecting efforts to set aside public funds for minority-owned businesses.[6] Much of the civil rights judicial arsenal currently is directed to modes of implementation and the effectiveness of the remedies applied.

The Court's responses at times have led to some confusion, but the overall effect has been at least a partial victory for civil rights advocates. In one instance, a majority declined to lend validity to a district court's resort to the contempt power as a means of compelling members of a local governing body to comply with judicial orders intended to effectuate housing desegregation remedies.[7] In another, the Court showed no similar qualms in upholding the exercise of judicial power to order a school district to increase property taxes at a rate appropriate to fund a desegregation plan.[8] Subsequently, the Justices established guidelines designed to release school districts from judicial desegregation decrees when good-faith compliance has been demonstrated and the "vestiges of past discrimination" have been eliminated "as far as practicable."[9] But fundamental precedents were reaffirmed, and the fabric of school integration litigation remained intact.

If the Rehnquist Court's decisions have evinced any conspicuous turnabouts, these have occurred in the area of the criminal law and, less emphatically, in rulings predicated upon the religion clauses of the First Amendment. Apart from long-term developments narrowing the exclusionary rule and affecting standards in capital punishment cases, substantial restrictions have been placed upon the availability of federal habeas corpus relief for prisoners held in custody.[10] The principal deviations distinguishing religion clause cases relate to historic guarantees of free exercise. Whether, following the Court's rejection of such claims in a Native American peyotist case,[11] similar judicial responses can be expected more generally restricting liberty of religious conscience remains problematic and may raise fundamental questions yet unforeseen.

On balance, the case law reflects a resolutely conservative Court superficially more quiescent than in the past, perhaps minimally less prone to intrude when the political branches have expressed themselves decisively, but a Court whose disavowed activism is difficult to conceal. The arid debate over "original intent" persists, and the results, despite the spirited rhetoric, remain as inconclusive as ever. In the practical idiom of judicial politics, constitutional relativism prevails as it has since the beginning of the Republic. And it is this traditional relativism that has given rise to a constant level of judicial intervention, albeit intermittent, but as compelling and controversial as it has been in the past. The Rehnquist Court, in some respects, has assumed an identity of its own. A reasonably coherent and consistent working majority exists to provide the basis for the Court often to function as a unit and to offer directional clues to the future course that it may pursue. But departures do occur and, on occasion, as in the 1992 abortion rights case,[12] there is unmistakable evidence of a centrist coalition that may control the outcome in critical areas of decision making.

NOTES

1. Texas v. Johnson, 491 U.S. 397 (1989); United States v. Eichman, 496 U.S. 310 (1990).
2. *See, e.g.*, Eisenstadt v. Baird, 405 U.S. 438 (1972) and Carey v. Population Services International, 431 U.S. 678 (1977).
3. *See* Stanley H. Friedelbaum, *A New Bill of Rights: Novel Dimensions of Liberty and Property, in* CIVIL LIBERTIES: POLICY AND POLICY MAKING ch. 9 (Stephen L. Wasby, ed., 1976).
4. Cruzan v. Director, Missouri Dept. of Health, 497 U.S. 261 (1990).
5. Metro Broadcasting, Inc. v. FCC, 497 U.S. 547 (1990).
6. City of Richmond v. J. A. Croson Co., 488 U.S. 469 (1989).
7. Spallone v. United States, 493 U.S. 265 (1990).
8. Missouri v. Jenkins, 495 U.S. 33 (1990).
9. Board of Education of Oklahoma Public Schools v. Dowell, 112 L. Ed. 2d 715 (1991).
10. Teague v. Lane, 489 U.S. 288 (1989).
11. Employment Division, Dept. of Human Resources v. Smith, 494 U.S. 872 (1990).
12. Planned Parenthood of Southeastern Pennsylvania v. Casey, 120 L. Ed. 2d 674 (1992).

THE
REHNQUIST COURT

—————————————— 1 ——————————————

The Status of Federalism

American federalism, at times the object of admiration though more
often of disparagement, has been a source of instability and strife
through much of the nation's history. In *Federalist* 45, James
Madison predicted that the national government's powers would be
"few and defined"; that the state's authority would extend to all of
the essential objects touching upon the personal concerns, internal
order, and prosperity of the populace; and that the federal government, owing its existence to the favor of the states, would be so
dependent as to "beget a disposition too obsequious than too
overbearing towards them." He went on to suggest in a succeeding
number that the "natural attachments" of the people would gravitate
to the states.

On a less positive note, Madison adverted to the "disposition and
the faculty" of the national and state governments to "resist and
frustrate the measures of each other." It was the latter conflict and
the slow but unremitting drift of power to the center that gave rise
to highly charged controversies culminating in the Civil War and
its turbulent aftermath. Beyond the stark drama of rebellion, seces-
sion, and reconstruction lay continuing differences, both of sub-

stance and of emphasis that led to a sporadic series of cases in later years continuing to describe and to clarify with greater exactness the nature of the states, of the Union, and of the ties and relationships that bound the fragile fabric together.

More closely linked to contemporary patterns of American federalism were recurring questions resulting from the adoption of the Fourteenth Amendment, especially chameleonic notions of due process and the substantive shapes and forms that it came to assume. The nationalization of the economy encouraged a legislative resort to regulatory measures which, in turn, were the subjects of increasingly intrusive judicial review. Such fictional inventions as liberty of contract and affectation with a public interest served as the precursors of a wave of judicial negativism unparalleled in the annals of the Republic. As late as the era of the Great Depression, the Supreme Court maintained a course of negative activism and interventionism so extreme as to threaten the institutional integrity of the Court. Political pressures heightened as the Court embraced rigorous, previously unknown standards of delegability as well as restrictions upon the national police power traditionally founded in the congressional commerce and taxation clauses. The Tenth Amendment was cited for the proposition that the reserved powers and quasi-sovereignty of the states had to be preserved at all costs against national incursions that were said to endanger accepted notions of dual federalism.

As economic due process receded from consideration as a viable option and, in fact, was well-nigh abandoned in the decisional turnabout that followed the 1937–38 Court-packing episode, so the strictures of delegability and Tenth Amendment restraints virtually disappeared from the Court's adjudicatory arsenal. Deference to the will of Congress and of the state legislatures reigned supreme. The Commerce Clause reemerged as a reminder of the plenary power to which Chief Justice John Marshall had referred in *Gibbons v. Ogden*,[1] though the breadth and reach of the taxation power was never afforded a like compass. Judicial neutrality or purposeful self-abnegation replaced negation. Interventionism was limited to exceptional occasions when due process was haltingly resurrected to advance libertarian interests.

With few exceptions, adherence to the principle of judicial deference prevailed for almost half a century. The Court's decision to set aside a state statute on equal protection grounds occurred late in the 1950s,[2] but the case was subsequently overruled amidst reaffirmations of a posture of nonintervention as it related to economic and social regulatory legislation.[3] Notions of judicial inaction became commonplace even as personnel changes came to pass and the so-called Roosevelt Court eventually served as no more than a vestige of the past rather than a functional entity. That total abdication never reached an all-encompassing level is evident from a critical and searching examination of judicial proceedings. Tersely revealed was the periodic resort to such alternative modes as findings of federal preemptive intent, limited revivals of the contract clause, narrow statutory construction, and notably less bland applications of traditional rationality tests.[4] Nonetheless, despite these departures from the norm, it was difficult to characterize the Court's attitude in terms other than deferential. Occasional returns to what seemed to approach meaningful review were hardly ascendant or highly consequential events.

It is perhaps not coincidental that the origins of the first successful challenge to an expansive federal police power originated from questions raised in relation to the Fair Labor Standards Act of 1938 and its extension to state employees. In its origins, the law reflected and carried forward wage-hour controversies dating from the early decades of the twentieth century when federal child labor statutes were held unconstitutional whether pursued by way of the commerce or taxation clauses.[5] If, then, the police power of Congress was sustained in relation to the private sector,[6] the attempted application of such standards to the states as employers prompted a revival of Tenth Amendment inquiries concerning reserved powers and their amenability to federal regulatory control. The legacy of the past had not been completely eradicated even as the post-1937 Court proceeded to categorize the Tenth Amendment as no more than a "truism that all is retained which has not been surrendered."[7] Notions of intergovernmental immunities, if less compelling than previously thought, continued to interject some significance in the federal-state equation.

When, in 1966, Congress extended provisions of the Fair Labor Standards Act to employees of state schools and hospitals, questions arose concerning the extent of "interference" permissible when state functions were affected. Justice John M. Harlan, sustaining the amendments for a divided Court in *Maryland v. Wirtz*,[8] rejected arguments that the commerce power must yield to claims of state soverignty. The state as an employer is subject to the same restrictions, Justice Harlan averred, "as a wide range of other employers whose activities affect commerce, including privately operated schools and hospitals." All the same, the Court was troubled by Tenth and Eleventh Amendment considerations and, with respect to the latter, it took the unusual step of reserving judgment. Justice William Douglas, joined in dissent by Justice Potter Stewart, asserted that in this instance the state as a sovereign power was "being seriously tampered with, potentially crippled."[9]

That the Tenth Amendment continued to display elements of vitality was evidenced once again in 1975 as the Court affirmed the validity of wage-price controls in a curious setting since the act of Congress authorizing such controls had already expired. In *Fry v. United States*,[10] Justice Thurgood Marshall made reference to *Wirtz* as a basis for foreclosing arguments alleging unwanted interference with sovereign state functions. By way of a footnote, he went on to cite the "truism" aphorism regarding the Tenth Amendment though placed in a context with seemingly little effective impact. In contrast to earlier and oft-repeated allusions to the Commerce Clause as a source of unlimited authority, Justice Marshall denied that Congress could exercise power in a fashion that "impairs the States' integrity or their ability to function effectively in a federal system."[11]

Justice William Rehnquist, dissenting in *Fry*, would have established more explicit state boundaries constitutionally unassailable and presumably safeguarded from federal intrusions.[12] Indeed, he would have set aside many of the basic tenets sustained in *Wirtz*. Justice Rehnquist avowed an "affirmative" right of a state, "inherent in its capacity as a [s]tate," and implicit in a system of constitutional federalism that might limit national power under the Commerce Clause.[13]

Recurrent hints of renewed attention to the Tenth Amendment as a preserver of state interests attained fulfillment the following year in *National League of Cities v. Usery*.[14] At issue were 1974 amendments to the wage and hour provisions of the Fair Labor Standards Act that extended to all employees of the states and their political subdivisions with the exception of executive, administrative, and professional personnel. Despite the breadth of congressional action under the Commerce Clause, a federal district court had dismissed claims of constitutional invalidity though the court apparently was troubled and had reached its conclusion reluctantly and solely on the strength of *Wirtz*. The latter impediment subsequently was eliminated when, in *National League of Cities*, Justice Rehnquist, writing for a sorely divided Supreme Court, overruled *Wirtz*. He alluded approvingly to Justice William Douglas' objections in his *Wirtz* dissent to permitting the national government to "devour the essentials of state sovereignty."[15]

The prevailing opinion in *National League of Cities* prepared the way for a return to some semblance of moderation in the federal-state balance, albeit one hardly akin to an equipoise in an era unmistakably and persistently dominated by a centripetal impetus. Justice Rehnquist differentiated congressional power to regulate commerce in regard to individuals or corporations from treatment of the states as states. The latter, in their sovereign capacity, were said to be beyond legislative reach since, in this instance, the wage-hour amendments operated directly to "displace the [s]tates' freedom to structure integral operations in areas of traditional governmental functions."[16] As Justice Rehnquist perceived it, even if an enactment fell within the scope of authority contained in the Commerce Clause, the offense might still be an invasion of Tenth Amendment rights. As the commerce power could not violate provisions of the Bill of Rights, so it might not intrude upon the reserved powers of the states.

These basic arguments, challenging excesses in Congress' exercise of the police power, were not wholly unanticipated in the light of earlier resorts to narrow statutory construction. The *Rewis-Bass* guidelines[17] had suggested limitations on the commerce power when it adversely affected or altered the federal-state relationship or impinged upon individual rights, particularly in relation to criminal law sanctions. Unless Congress conveyed its purpose and intent with clarity, Justice Marshall had warned, "it will not be deemed to have significantly changed the Federal-State balance."[18] A flurry of comparably narrow readings of statutory language also occurred within an antitrust law context,[19] raising charges of a pro-big business bias.

In view of the Court's previously held misgivings, though expressed by way of statutory construction, Justice Brennan's irate reaction to the majority opinion in *National League of Cities* almost defied credibility. Much in the manner of a stalwart combatant, he took exception to what he termed the majority's creation of an "abstraction without substance" lacking either grounding in the Constitution or in precedent. He reminded his colleagues of the dangers that lurked in an "overly restrictive" construction of the commerce power—one that had previously threatened the standing of the Court.

Justice Brennan went on to extol the virtues of the political process as a safeguard for state interests as distinguished from an "unacceptable" return to judicial supervision. In vigorous prose, Brennan assailed the "catastrophic judicial body blow" dealt congressional authority and the "ominous portent of disruption" implicit in this "mischievous" decision. Throughout the polemic, it appears, Justice Brennan was aware of his penchant for hyperbole concerning an opinion more closely confined in its reach than he was willing to concede. He did admit that Congress could readily achieve the objectives sought by conditioning grants of federal funds on state compliance with federally mandated wage and overtime standards.[20]

All the same, Justice Brennan and his dissenting colleagues undertook what seems in retrospect to have been a purposeful campaign to circumvent and eventually to overturn *National League of Cities*. If the crafting of the contours of American federalism remained in limbo, there were continuing, if artful, efforts made to remold the formulas that had been fashioned. A pre-enforcement challenge to a major regulatory scheme, encompassing a nationwide program to protect society and the environment from the detrimental effects of surface coal mining, called into question many of the Tenth Amendment limitations developed in *National League of Cities.* Justice Marshall, writing for a unanimous Court in *Hodel v. Virginia Surface Mining and Reclamation Assn.*,[21] sustained the statute on traditional Commerce Clause grounds, carefully taking into account and addressing charges predicated on an invasion of reserved state powers. Deference to the express findings of Congress took on a renewed significance and, in the circumstances, the means selected were said to be "reasonable and appropriate."[22]

Claims linked to the regulation of states as states failed, Justice Marshall averred in *Hodel,* since pertinent provisions of the act affected the activities of mine operators who were private entrepreneurs, not agents of the state. In addition, Justice Marshall noted, there could be no suggestion that the act "commandeer[ed]" the legislative processes of the states or compelled enforcement of the statute. Cooperative federalism did not constitute coercion. Nor was there any threat of federal usurpation of the regulatory roles of the states. To the contrary, Justice Marshall declared, congressional power under the Commerce Clause could preempt state-law determinations contrary to the results sought in the federal plan.[23] Yet Justice Rehnquist, while concurring in the judgment, cautioned that the federal system did not exist "only at the sufferance of Congress" and that, despite the breadth of holdings under the Commerce Clause, constitutional limits did exist in relation to exercises of the regulatory power.[24]

Perhaps the Court came closest to overturning *National League of Cities* when, in 1983, it sustained the 1974 extension of the definition of an "employer" under the Age Discrimination in Employment Act to include state and local governments. At issue in *EEOC v. Wyoming*[25] was a complaint filed with the Equal Employment Opportunity Commission by a state fish and game warden who had been required to retire at age 55 under the applicable state statute and regulations. A federal district court had held the extension unconstitutional in response to an enforcement action initiated by the EEOC. The Supreme Court found to the contrary in an adroit restatement, actually a rewriting, of *National League of Cities.*

Justice Brennan, writing the majority opinion for the Court by reason of Justice Blackmun's change of vote, turned to the application of the three-pronged test formulated in *National League of Cities*. He found no cause to invalidate Congress' extension of the provisions of the Age Discrimination in Employment Act to state and local employees. That the act regulated the states as states was not seriously disputed. But, even if the mandatory retirement proviso involved an exercise of state sovereignty, Brennan asserted, it did not "directly impair" the ability of the state to "structure integral operations" with respect to traditional governmental functions. The degree of federal intrusiveness was said to be sufficiently less serious than it was in *National League of Cities*. Consequently, Justice Brennan argued, it was not necessary to deny Congress' power in respect to the exercise of its regulatory function.[26] That Justice Brennan's opinion approached a de facto overturning of the core elements found in *National League of Cities* seems evident from the superficial distinctions that he described to set apart the scheme under review in *EEOC V. Wyoming*. Brennan's claim that the extension act provisions would have neither a direct nor an obvious negative impact on state finances is difficult to accept. Chief Justice Warren Burger, joined in dissent by Justices Powell, Rehnquist, and O'Connor, characterized the reserved powers of the states as having been "turned on their heads" when federal age standards were made applicable to state law enforcement officers. In effect, the Chief Justice insisted, Congress had been permitted to compel the states to conduct their internal affairs in conformity with a "national mold" without respect to local needs and conditions.[27]

If the demise of *National League of Cities* appeared to be imminent, it was surprising that, when it occurred, the Court elected to resort to a decidedly unimpressive case as the vehicle for setting aside a precedent less than a decade old. *Garcia v. San Antonio Metropolitan Transit Authority*[28] was not a likely choice in view of the locus of those who claimed coverage under the terms of the Fair Labor Standards Act extension. They were employed by an agency not directly associated with nor essentially required to function as a vehicle of state government. Little ingenuity was needed to establish that the transit authority did not lie within any cognizable category that would ineluctably immunize it from the reach of congressional authority under the Commerce Clause. Thus, had judicial review followed its usual course, the wage-hour provisions could have been given effect without disturbing the intrinsically precarious and limited framework so recently created.

Instead, Justice Blackmun, whose "swing" vote had made the critical difference affecting the outcome of the *Wyoming* case, was selected to write for the Court in a manner that touched upon the fundamental nature of American federalism. From the outset, he rejected any reliance upon the governmental/proprietary dichotomy as a means of resolving the conflict with minimally disturbing effects. To the contrary, he took the occasion to denounce as "unsound in principle and unworkable in practice" any rule attempting to preclude federal regulatory power premised on a judicial appraisal denoting particular functions as "integral" or "traditional." Such a rule, Justice Blackmun argued, disserved democratic principles and bred "inconsistency" because it was torn asunder from those principles.[29]

Moving to the central themes expounded in *National League of Cities*, Justice Blackmun declined to embrace what he termed "freestanding conceptions" of state sovereignty when weighed against such mainstays of regulatory power as the Commerce Clause. State interests, he went on to note, were secured by "procedural safeguards" deriving from the structure of federalism, not by judicially devised restrictions on national power. Restraints must be fashioned to offset "possible failings" in the national political process rather than to delineate a "sacred province" of state autonomy. In the final analysis, Blackmun argued, the national political process assured that excessively onerous impediments would not be placed upon the states. The continued vitality of the states did not require any reliance on the model identified in *National League of Cities*—a model that Justice Blackmun called "both impracticable and doctrinally barren." Consequently, although admittedly of recent date, the case was overruled.[30]

The dissenting opinions assailed what each, in turn, took to be major inroads upon the constitutional foundations of American federalism. Justice Lewis Powell, joined by Chief Justice Burger and Justices Rehnquist and O'Connor, wrote of the reduction of the Tenth Amendment to "meaningless rhetoric" when Congress acts under the Commerce Clause. Judicial review, Justice Powell charged, was being made to yield to political decision making in redefining the status of federalism. In doing so, two centuries of "understanding[s]" were being set aside.[31]

Justice Sandra Day O'Connor, joined by Justices Powell and Rehnquist, expressed her disagreement with the majority's view of federalism and of the Court's responsibilities as an ultimate reviewing agency. Within an integrated national economy, Congress had been accorded a "breathtaking" expansion of its powers, particularly in actions attributable to the Commerce Clause. Yet Justice O'Connor denied that whatever remained of state sovereignty ought to be committed solely to the protection of the political process. Safeguards, if any continued to exist, lay with the Court; and she admonished her colleagues that, despite the overruling of *National League of Cities*, they should not be left to Congress, a body that had often demonstrated its "underdeveloped capacity for self-restraint." An appeal to the "essence" of federalism, Justice O'Connor declared, would not suffice in guarding against a unitary, centralized national government.[32]

Justice Rehnquist, dissenting, joined Justice O'Connor in the belief that the Court in time would reassume its appropriate responsibilities and set aside *Garcia*.[33] That this has not come to pass, regardless of changing personnel, is surprising, if not disconcerting. It is possible that the cases presented for review have not provided a suitable vehicle. Or, perhaps more likely, the recent appointees, Justices Scalia, Kennedy, and Souter, have not evinced sufficient enthusiasm to set aside *Garcia*, whether by reason of a reluctance to transgress shaky principles of stare decisis or a disinclination to curtail the reach of the commerce power. In any event, without any cogently identifiable challenge, Justice Blackmun's opinion in *Garcia* has led to predictable results: a further "deconstitutionalization" of the Commerce Clause; a renewed retreat from the Tenth Amendment as a viable predicate; major inroads threatening, even precluding, any expectations of a vibrant federalism; and a continuing departure from judicial review in a Court already dominated by repeated resorts to an unremitting doctrine of deference in the regulatory area.

When, in 1987, an occasion arose for a possible reexamination of *Garcia*, an attenuated context, coupled with the changed character of the congressional power advanced, served to diminish any likelihood that the 1985 decision would be reconsidered. The case, *South Dakota v. Dole*,[34] directed attention to the spending power of Congress with no more than ancillary references to the Commerce Clause. Enactment of the National Minimum Drinking Age Amendment of 1984 required the withholding of a percentage of federal highway funds from states that failed to ban persons under 21 years old from purchasing or possessing alcoholic beverages. South Dakota refused to comply, permitting 19-year-olds to purchase beer containing up to 3.2 percent alcohol. The state challenged the condition and penalty sought to be imposed as ranging beyond the spending power and as violative of state prerogatives guaranteed by the Twenty-first Amendment. Although there were incidental references to the Tenth Amendment, it was apparent that the primary focus lay elsewhere.

Chief Justice Rehnquist, writing for the Court, sustained the law despite the state's contention that the conditional grants exceeded the scope of the spending power. A majority noted that Congress had acted in pursuit of the "general welfare"; that it had done so unambiguously; and that its stated conditions were related to a national concern, that is, to ensure safe interstate travel. The chief justice denied that anyone's constitutional rights had been violated. Nor might the conditional grant proviso be independently barred by such exceptions as those found in the Twenty-first Amendment. The limitations on Congress when it acts under the spending power, Rehnquist noted, are "less exacting" than those applicable when the regulatory power is being exercised directly. And, the Court concluded, because the penalty imposed was minimal, the argument of coercion in derogation of state sovereignty was "more rhetoric than fact."[35]

Justices Brennan and O'Connor dissented on the basis of the Twenty-first Amendment's reservations of power to the states. In fact, Justice O'Connor went beyond the terse wording of Brennan's disagreement with the Court. While agreeing with much of the majority's exposition of the spending power, she took issue with the proposition that conditional grants might be used to alter regulations in state social and economic areas because of tangential linkages to highway safety or use. Justice O'Connor insisted that Congress' commerce power could not be resorted to in this instance because of the Twenty-first Amendment and the protective cover that it had superimposed. In the absence of the amendment, O'Connor seemed to concede, a "strong" argument could have been made that Congress might extend its regulatory authority under the Commerce Power to the sale of intoxicating liquors as it had to many other commodities.[36]

Clearly, *Garcia* suffered minimally if at all as a result of the South Dakota ruling. Apart from Justice O'Connor's opinion, little was said concerning the status of federalism; and even her review lacked any real fervor. The impetus was missing in relation to the artifice of conditional grants as distinguished from a direct reliance on the regulatory power. With notably minor emphasis on Tenth Amendment strictures, the Twenty-first Amendment might have served as a formidable barrier to protect the states. Justice Brennan, it needs to be recalled, wrote in support of the amendment as a state power-preserving mechanism—one that struck the "proper balance" between national and state power. Yet Chief Justice Rehnquist apparently was not persuaded to attach controlling authority to the Twenty-first Amendment as a source protective of state sovereignty. Indeed, the absence of significant Tenth Amendment constraints, juxtaposed in opposition to congressional regulatory power under the Commerce Clause, reduced the South Dakota case to a subordinate doctrinal level—one that made it unsuitable for a meaningful reappraisal, much less a reversal, of *Garcia*.

More closely linked to the doctrinal guidelines developed in *Garcia* were questions that arose three years later in *South Carolina v. Baker*.[37] A long-term precedent shielded from federal income taxation the interest derived by individuals from bonds issued by state and local governments. Immunity had been accorded a constitutionally protected status since 1895 when, in *Pollock v. Farmers' Loan & Trust Co.*,[38] the Supreme Court held that such a levy could not be imposed since it constituted a direct tax on the state. Undeniably, over a period of almost a century that had intervened, doctrines of intergovernmental immunities had been markedly narrowed as the Court moved to sustain an array of tax sources. Previous notions of dual federalism, differentiating exclusive spheres of federal and state authority, were abandoned in favor of an interactive or "cooperative" federalism. The search for additional revenues was pursued with great vigor during the era of the Great Depression and the years that followed. What was left of immunity converged about the core elements of sovereignty, that is, essential functions and activities peculiar to the states as states and to the nation. It remained to be determined whether the last vestiges of federal-state duality—the constitutional nontaxability of interest payable on state and local bonds—were to be afforded a special status apart from earnings accruing from other contractual obligations. The latter, contemporary case law counseled, were vulnerable to taxation for want of a constitutionally secured shelter.

The mechanism that triggered a reassessment of the status of interest on state and local bonds lay in legislation passed in 1982. As a part of a major tax revision effort, Congress had sought to eliminate bearer bonds that, it was claimed, often encouraged tax evasion because the income was unreported and difficult to trace. The new law required issuance of bonds registered in the names of the owners if the exemption was to be maintained. As the Court viewed the consequences of the congressional scheme, it was clear that the statute not only provided powerful incentives for registered bonds; in effect, the act banned bearer bonds as much as if the prohibition had been explicit. Clearly, it was this unmistakable objective that brought South Carolina before the Supreme Court, thereby invoking the Court's original jurisdiction.

The state's challenges reflected a broadly based amalgam, ranging from purported violations of the Tenth Amendment, principles of federalism, and intergovernmental immunities to the teachings and latter-day significance of *Garcia*. Justice Brennan wrote for the Court, rejecting all of the charges of constitutional infirmity leveled by the state. If *Garcia* left open any avenue for invalidation on the basis of the Tenth Amendment, it had been effectively closed, he averred, in the absence of "extraordinary defects in the national political process." Courts were not free to second-guess the substantive basis for legislation by probing into the decision-making process or by defining areas of "unregulable" state activity.[39]

The majority went on to overrule *Pollock* as well as to cite a series of so-called contractor cases[40] for the proposition that the taxation of private parties doing business with the national government did not offend the Constitution even if the economic burden fell on the United States. Justice Brennan made plain that the only remaining exception to the general rule was the immunity accorded recipients of bond interest. This exception, as he perceived it, could only be explained by the historical fact that Congress had precluded taxation of state interest by statute dating from the first income tax law passed in 1913. Apart from the legislative exemption, Brennan concluded, state bond owners "have no constitutional entitlement not to pay taxes on income they earn from state bonds, and States have no constitutional entitlement to issue bonds paying lower interest rates than other issuers."[41]

In concurring opinions, Chief Justice Rehnquist and Justice Scalia disclaimed any association with the majority's assertions that the only constitutional protection afforded the states is to be found in the national political process. Rehnquist, in particular, would have limited the opinion to the "well-supported conclusion" that the act of 1982 had no more than a minimal impact on the states and that it met the standard espoused in *National League of Cities* forbidding any displacement of the states' freedom to structure integral operations in traditional areas. Beyond such a determination, the Chief Justice noted, the issues explored need best be left unaddressed.[42]

Justice O'Connor's dissenting opinion returned to many of the substantive questions treated in *Garcia*. She opted to delve far more intensively than Rehnquist and Scalia would have preferred into the nature of federalism and the components that underlay it. Referring to the "devastating effects" and the "erosion" of state sovereignty that would result from federal taxation of state bond interest, Justice

O'Connor eschewed a sole reliance on congressionally sanctioned immunity. The autonomy of the state, she argued, should rest on the Tenth Amendment, established principles of federalism, and the Guarantee Clause of the Constitution to protect against possible incursions. In sum, Justice O'Connor charged, the Court had failed to meet its responsibilities to enforce the constitutional safeguards of "state autonomy and self-sufficiency" that might otherwise be jeopardized.[43]

In retrospect, what appeared to be a likely vehicle for a major alteration or even a partial repudiation of *Garcia* proved to be a peripheral ruling at best. The issues raised in *Baker* touched upon many of the significant elements essential to a reassessment of American federalism. Yet, as Chief Justice Rehnquist intimated, the 1982 legislation met the tests prescribed in intergovernmental immunities cases of the past half century. Bondholders were not unlike private contractors. Taxes imposed upon interest derived from public bonds were no more levied upon the states as states than they were imposed upon the profits derived from private sales to the national government and its agencies. Doubtless Rehnquist would have liked to revive *National League of Cities*, but the circumstances and the justices prone to do so were not available to these ends. Justice Scalia might have been persuaded to join, albeit less enthusiastically, had the conditions been suitable. Whether Justice Kennedy, who did not participate in the South Carolina case, would have provided an additional vote remains problematic. In future cases, much may depend on Justice Souter, one of the Court's recent appointees and a former associate justice of the New Hampshire Supreme Court. If and when *Garcia* is set aside or substantially modified, the question recurs, will constitutional federalism be restored to what the majority in *National League of Cities* conceived to be its historic role, or will congressional federalism survive as it has for half a century, especially when taken in concert with an expansive federal police power premised on the Commerce Clause?

The fervor associated with debates over the nature of American federalism and its structural underpinnings is not evident in other significant but less compelling issue areas. Dormant Commerce

Clause cases have raised important and often intricate questions regarding economic protectionism and state taxation affecting interstate commerce. Ancillary issues relate to appropriate apportionment formulas and cumulative tax burdens.[44] Beyond the commerce power lie provocative queries concerning federal preemption and its underlying rationale, whether linked to statutory construction, the Supremacy Clause of Article VI of the Constitution, or policy considerations less explicitly revealed. Deference to state determinations in both sectors has continued to prevail, albeit at times in theory. Occasionally, the balance in the federal system has turned against the states even as the national government's actions project an outward mien of restraint and permissiveness. The issues treated address basic concerns touching upon federal-state relations, but the emotive force of *National League of Cities*, *Garcia*, and succeeding cases is missing, though hardly inconsequential.

The doctrine of a negative or dormant Commerce Clause dates from the mid-nineteenth century when the Court embraced a compromise formula that suggested the exercise of federal-state concurrent powers under the Clause.[45] Considerable causes of controversy remained, particularly in relation to state taxation of businesses engaged in interstate commerce. By contemporary standards, any levy is required to be nondiscriminatory, fairly apportioned, not imposing a multiple tax burden, and in compliance with due process nexus guidelines sufficiently linking the out-of-state taxpayer to localized activities and transactions. In *Northwestern States Portland Cement Co. v. Minnesota*,[46] the court assumed a need to clear away the "tangled underbrush" of past cases in an area that had developed "like Topsy." While acknowledging that the states may not be permitted "one single-tax-worth of direct interference with the free flow of commerce,"[47] Justice Tom C. Clark, who wrote for the majority, went on to afford the states great breadth in imposing net income taxes on out-of-state corporations. Justice Felix Frankfurter, in dissent, took exception to what he conceived to be judicial acquiesence in undue impediments obstructing the free flow of trade between the states.

Such opposing philosophies continue to be characteristic of cases in the Rehnquist Court. Justice Stevens, who wrote for the Court in *Tyler Pipe Industries v. Washington Department of Revenue*,[48] found a state business and occupation tax violative of the Commerce Clause by reason of a "multiple activities" exemption. By contrast, Justice Scalia warned against invoking the Commerce Clause as a "self-operative check" on state legislation.[49] He cautioned that the language of the Clause provided no indication of "exclusivity," and that persistent resorts to the negative Commerce Clause have not always been justifiable.[50] Yet Justice Scalia, for a unanimous Court in a subsequent case, applied the Clause's "negative" aspect to a state tax credit scheme found to be discriminatory against interstate commerce[51]—in effect, a prohibited form of economic protectionism, that is, "regulatory measures designed to benefit in-state economic interests by burdening out-of-state competitors."[52] "Plain" discrimination, Scalia concluded, could not be sustained by way of a reciprocity plan, the justifications of which amounted to "no more than implausible speculation."[53]

That the Supreme Court has not embarked upon a campaign to hold the states to a strict accounting in the imposition of taxes affecting interstate commerce may not be readily apparent from the leading cases. But these are atypical by dint of circumstances; they represent a departure from a generally deferential pattern referred to in the deviant opinions. The Court has been careful to adhere to broad guidelines serving to uphold most state levies unless they fall into narrowly defined categories markedly contrary to time-honored principles supportive of a free national market. Justice Scalia, a continuing critic of the dormant Commerce Clause and its applications, stresses the need to accord the states an "appropriate degree of freedom to structure their revenue measures." He takes exception to judicially fashioned rules that are excessively restrictive of state powers and that are premised on an "unstable structure" which, viewed over the expanse of more than a century, "made no sense."[54]

To a greater degree than criteria governing state taxation affecting commerce, preemption doctrines often reflect not only perceptions of federalism but also policy determinations at times paralleling substantive due process decisions. Traditionally, preemption has developed within the contours of commerce clause litigation, but this has not been obligatory for at least the past half century. A cluster of cases during the Warren years extended to such diverse areas as sedition[55] and labor-management relations[56] with preemption or supersedure vaguely disguising judicial policy objectives linked to substantive considerations and designs. Indeed, federal preemption reached such heights that bills were introduced in Congress (and nearly approved) to reverse a "nationally-oriented" presumption unless Congress specifically so provides or the federal-state conflict is direct and positive. The Civil Rights Act of 1964 contained an anti-preemptive proviso intended to ensure that earlier state civil rights laws, accompanied by extensive histories and impressive precedents, would not be cavalierly set aside.

Preemption cases, like other major forays into judicial policy-making, reflect a broad array of societal problems and issues. The decisions range widely into a host of areas that have attracted the attention of state legislatures and agencies as well as of Congress and the federal bureaucracy. Findings of federal-state coordination of efforts or overt conflict do not follow clear-cut patterns or lines of demarcation. Arguments in behalf of one or another outcome, in many instances, are rarely conclusive, categorical, or drawn determinately from the decisional repository. Instead, much depends upon result orientation tied, more often than not, to the predilections and prevailing value preferences of the judges.

A much-publicized preemption dispute juxtaposed provisions of a state's fair employment law, extending leave and job reinstatement rights to pregnant employees, against Title VII of the federal Civil Rights Act of 1964 as amended by the Pregnancy Discrimination Act. In 1978, Congress had responded to an adverse Supreme Court decision holding that an employer not including pregnancy as a compensable disability, within the terms of an otherwise comprehensive insurance plan, did not violate Title VII's ban on sex discrimination.[57] The pregnancy act, passed as a remedial measure, specified that discrimination based on pregnancy constituted sex discrimination within the meaning of Title VII and that women so affected be treated for all employment-related purposes as are other persons similar in their ability or inability to work. It was noteworthy that Congress specifically disclaimed any intent to preempt state law or to "occupy the field" of employment discrimination.

All the same, a challenge filed by an employer in *California Federal Savings and Loan Assoc. v. Guerra*[58] charged that a counterpart state law, invoked by the complainant in this case, was inconsistent with and, therefore, preempted by Title VII as amended. The California act was said to have provided broader protection than the federal statute, requiring preferential treatment for female employees and disfavoring temporarily disabled males. Thus, it followed that discrimination against men had occurred in contravention of the federal scheme. A federal district court so ruled, but the court of appeals reversed on grounds that preemption was not a necessary result of the dual statutory framework. Instead, as the appeals courts conceived it, Congress had established a "floor" beneath which pregnancy disability benefits might not fall, not a ceiling limiting any appreciable enlargement.[59]

It was the latter approach to pregnancy rights that the Supreme Court elected to pursue in weighing the preemption issue. Justice Marshall, who wrote for the Court, made reference to the so-called "objective" tests of supersession derived from *Rice v. Santa Fe Elevator Corp.*[60] and succeeding cases. Having disposed of criteria that bore little or no relation to the legislation under review, the Court centered about the actual conflict theme. Was compliance with federal and state regulations physically impossible? Did the state law pose demonstrable obstacles to accomplishment of the purposes of Congress? Justice Marshall found no palpable inconsistencies; compliance with both statutes was possible. Employers remained at liberty to provide comparable benefits to disabled employees in addition to what was being extended to pregnant women.[61]

Despite these efforts to create the illusion of equivalency, two concurring opinions revealed underlying tensions. Justice Stevens took the majority opinion to mean that "some preferential treatment of pregnancy" was permissible. Stevens went on to reject the proposition that the federal act mandated complete neutrality and prohibited the beneficial treatment of pregnancy.[62] In a second concurring opinion, Justice Scalia, apparently troubled by the Court's lengthy and tortuous discourse, expressed a preference for a simple resolution of the preemption question. He purported to examine no more than the antipreemptive provisions of Title VII, of which the pregnancy act was a part. Since the state law did not require any refusal to accord equal treatment to others similarly situated, the benefits afforded pregnant women did not violate the federal act and no unlawful employment practice had occurred. "No more is needed," Scalia argued, in the decision of this case.[63]

Justice White, joined by Chief Justice Rehnquist and Justice Powell, dissented. The federal act, he averred, did not permit preferential treatment of pregnant workers since such conduct failed to comport with the equal treatment purposes and provisions of Title VII. The state law was in "square conflict" with the federal statute and, therefore, the former was preempted.[64] White's position, which he documented persistently by references to statutory language, was a persuasive one by reference to linguistic considerations though the prevailing majority doubtless took the textual allusions to be excessively and perhaps unrealistically literal in character.

A reliance on preemption doctrines as formidable sources in the judicial arsenal of precedents is doubtful at best and untrustworthy in anticipating the outcome of cases. The impact of corporate takeovers has been widely debated as a matter of economic theory and practice with concomitant repercussions in the political system. Where, as here, Congress has acted, presumably to protect the public interest, the interjection of state regulatory legislation has created controversy well beyond the usual concern over preemptive intent. As in gender-related cases, the federal-state relationship has become a part of a complex web of often conflicting components that touch upon the policy-making process. The stakes are high in the regulation of sophisticated dealings in the ever-fascinating and ever-changing annals of the nation's financial community.

In *CTS Corporation v. Dynamics Corporation of America*,[65] a fledgling Rehnquist Court had its first opportunity to review a state's anti-takeover statute and to assess its applicability in the light of a federal law covering similar issues. A divided Court, speaking through Justice Powell, sustained the state law against a corporation's charges that the local scheme was preempted by the Williams Act, a federal statute governing hostile corporate stock tender offers. The Williams Act was said to preclude and, in fact, to preempt state laws that had a divisive effect upon the precarious balance between so-called target company management and a tender offeror. In short, the question persistently arose, was the state to be permitted to intercede in an effort to prevent disruption of the local economy with attendant dislocating effects that went well beyond the equities markets? Alternatively, should state intervention be sustained, would this not be a blow to a free national economy and a move supporting both provincialism and protectionism?

Closely intertwined with these policy questions lay long-standing guidelines describing preemption, its force, its import, and its consequences. Justice Powell distinguished an earlier case[66] that had set aside a state anti-takeover law as contrary to the Williams Act. Powell pointed out that the plurality opinion in the preceding case was not binding but that, even if it were, the Indiana act in *CTS Corporation* would still "pass muster." The Court found that the act's delaying tactics with respect to tender offers did not compel a conclusion that the federal statute superseded it. Investor protection, the subject of the federal law, was enhanced by the Indiana Legislature in guarding against "coercive" offers. Had Congress intended to preempt all state laws that delay acquisition of corporate voting control, Justice Powell noted, it would have so stated explicitly in view of the long-standing prevalence of state regulation in this area.[67] Dormant Commerce Clause claims were also dismissed.

Separate opinions in *CTS Corporation* pointed to particular foibles not wholly dissimilar from those previously addressed, albeit in a different context, in *Guerra*. Justice Scalia, concurring, examined the statutes in question and detected no conflicting provisions. What is more, he opted in favor of state control over the structure of local corporations. In closing, Scalia explained that he did not share the majority's "apparent high estimation of the beneficence" of the state statute but, as he put it, a law can be "both economic folly and constitutional."[68]

Justice White, joined by Justices Blackmun and Stevens, dissented. White asserted that the Indiana law, by design, would "frustrate" individual investment decisions and disturb the "careful balance" created by the Williams Act. He went on to note that the state law was preempted by the federal statute. But, in arriving at this judgment, Justice White cited "practical impact" as the deciding factor in an assessment of the preemption issue. Additionally, a clear conflict with the Commerce Clause was said to exist as a significant factor in the decisional calculus.[69]

The American version of federalism, still one of the nation's major if not always most inventive contributions to the art of statecraft, has not revealed any marked alteration of course or purpose in the opening years of the Rehnquist Court. Instead, there are signals, some covert and others slightly more conspicuous, that suggest significant changes in the offing. If, with the departure of Justice Brennan, *Garcia* may be overruled in an appropriate case, an unimpaired return to *National League of Cities* and its configuration of formulas no longer seems to be assured. Recent appointees, especially Justice Scalia, do not appear to accept all of the trappings associated with a conservatively oriented Court. Should constitutional federalism reemerge as a paradigm of a power-distribution model, the contours may not match, with any degree of exactness, those set out in *National League of Cities* or in the preceding sequence of cases.

Nor is it clear that ancillary doctrines, subsumed within the supporting substructure of federalism, will develop according to previous patterns. The dormant Commerce Clause is no longer wholly reliable as a broad-ranging preserver of a free national market unless the indicators of state protectionism are unambiguous or blatant. In the area of preemption, elements of a vague, evasive simplicity have reappeared though the end-results sought to be achieved remain as significant and as policy-oriented (perhaps toward the attainment of different goals) as they have been in the past. In sum, efforts to define or to redefine the salient qualities of American federalism remain as elusive as ever except in regard to less pressing issues, like interstate rendition,[70] that are largely remnants of historic happenstance rather than current political debate.

As the Rehnquist Court continues to take on a distinctive identity, then, the safeguards of federalism may fail to reflect either constitutional or political attributes viewed as mutually preclusive protective shields. Instead, a mid-spectrum position is more likely to embody the findings of the Court. Advocates of a doctrine of deference (close to but not unremitting) may be prevailed upon to concede the existence of constitutional safeguards and even the role of the Tenth Amendment. Yet invocation of the amendment need not be as striking or as obvious as it was in *National League of Cities*. An "originalist" conception of national powers could err on the side of a broad-ranging regulatory authority, perhaps moderated by obscure allusions to residual state powers best left unstated. It is doubtful that Justices Rehnquist and O'Connor will realize the revival that each anticipated in their *Garcia* dissents.

NOTES

1. 9 Wheat. 1 (1824).
2. Morey v. Doud, 354 U.S. 457 (1957).
3. New Orleans v. Dukes, 427 U.S. 297 (1976).
4. *See* Stanley H. Friedelbaum, *Reprise or Denouement: Deference and the New Dissonance in the Burger Court*, 26 EMORY L.J. 337 (1977).
5. *See* Hammer v. Dagenhart, 247 U.S. 251 (1918) and Bailey v. Drexel Furniture Co., 259 U.S. 20 (1922).
6. United States v. Darby, 312 U.S. 100 (1941).
7. *Id.* at 124.
8. 392 U.S. 183 (1968).
9. *Id.* at 205.
10. 421 U.S. 542 (1975).
11. *Id.* at 547 n.7.
12. *Id.* at 550–51.
13. *Id.* at 553.
14. 426 U.S. 833 (1976).
15. *Id.* at 855.
16. *Id.* at 852.
17. Rewis v. United States, 401 U.S. 808 (1971); United States v. Bass, 404 U.S. 336 (1971).
18. 404 U.S. at 349.

19. *See, e.g.,* Gulf Oil Corp. v. Copp Paving Co., 419 U.S. 186 (1976).
20. 426 U.S. at 880.
21. 452 U.S. 264 (1981).
22. *Id.* at 283.
23. *Id.* at 291–92.
24. *Id.* at 308–10.
25. 460 U.S. 226 (1983).
26. *Id.* at 239.
27. *Id.* at 264–65.
28. 469 U.S. 528 (1985).
29. *Id.* at 546–47.
30. *Id.* at 554–57.
31. *Id.* at 560.
32. *Id.* at 580–89.
33. *Id.* at 579–80.
34. 483 U.S. 203 (1987).
35. *Id.* at 207–11.
36. *Id.* at 212–18.
37. 485 U.S. 505 (1988).
38. 157 U.S. 429 (1895).
39. 485 U.S. at 512–13.
40. *See, e.g.,* James v. Dravo Contracting Co., 302 U.S. 134 (1937); Alabama v. King & Boozer, 314 U.S. 1 (1941); United States v. City of Detroit, 355 U.S. 466 (1958).
41. 485 U.S. at 525.
42. *Id.* at 529–30.
43. *Id.* at 531–34. *Cf.* Justice O'Connor's opinion for the Court in New York v. United States, 120 L.Ed.2d 120 (1992).
44. *See, e.g.,* Walter Hellerstein, *Commerce Clause Restraints on State Taxation: Purposeful Economic Protectionism and Beyond,* 85 Mich. L. Rev. 758 (1987).
45. Cooley v. Board of Wardens, 12 How. 299 (1852).
46. 358 U.S. 450 (1959).
47. Freeman v. Hewit, 329 U.S. 249 (1946).
48. 483 U.S. 232 (1987).
49. *Id.* at 257.
50. *Id.* at 259–60. *Cf.* American Trucking Ass'ns v. Scheiner, 483 U.S. 266 (1987).
51. New Energy Co. of Ind. v. Limbach, 486 U.S. 269 (1988).
52. *Id.* at 273.
53. *Id.* at 280.
54. Tyler Pipe Indus. v. Washington Dep't of Revenue, 483 U.S. 232, 254 (1987). *See also* Justice Scalia's concurring opinions in Bendix Autolite Corp. v. Midwesco Enter., 486 U.S. 888, 895–98 (1988) and Goldberg v. Sweet, 488 U.S. 252, 271 (1989).

55. Pennsylvania v. Nelson, 350 U.S. 497 (1956).
56. Guss v. Utah Labor Relations Bd., 353 U.S. 1 (1957); San Diego Bldg.
Trades Council v. Garmon, 359 U.S. 236 (1959).
57. General Electric Co. v. Gilbert, 429 U.S. 125 (1976). *See also* Nashville
Gas Co. v. Satty, 434 U.S. 136 (1977).
58. 479 U.S. 272 (1987).
59. *Id.* at 285.
60. 331 U.S. 218 (1947).
61. California Sav. and Loan Ass'n. v. Guerra, 479 U.S. 272, 290–91 (1987).
62. *Id.* at 294–95.
63. *Id.* at 295–96.
64. *Id.* at 298.
65. 481 U.S. 69 (1987).
66. Edgar v. MITE Corp., 457 U.S. 624 (1982).
67. CTS Corporation v. Dynamics Corp. of Am., 481 U.S. 69, 86 (1987).
68. *Id.* at 96–97.
69. *Id.* at 99, 101.
70. *See* Puerto Rico v. Branstad, 483 U.S. 219 (1987), overruling Kentucky
v. Dennison, 24 How. 66 (1861), in relation to the power of federal courts to
compel governors to fulfill obligations incumbent upon them under the Extradition Clause of Article IV of the Constitution.

2

Liberty and Privacy Interests: A Search for Rationalizing Principles

The Rehnquist Court, like its predecessors, has directed attention to due process liberty concepts as well as to cognate definitions of privacy and personal autonomy. Such efforts have been evident in a number of decisions of the past several years, increasingly cast in negative terms. Debates concerning "original intent" continue to arise from time to time as the Court grapples with elusive questions of privacy that have long defied resolution. Like allied conflicts over constitutional relativism, the resultant dialogue has often become an exercise in semantics more closely tied to vacuous disputation than to the realities of judicial politics. A majority of the contemporary Court, either expressly or tacitly, seems to accept, however grudgingly, minimal responsibility to adapt the Constitution, including formative guarantees of liberty and privacy, to the societal needs and contingencies of the last decade of the twentieth century. What remains controversial and open to persistent inquiry are the ways of justifying the ends reached and the selection of appropriate tools of implementation.

Notions of liberty derive from a lengthy historical record, linked to characterizations of due process developed over a period spanning several centuries. If, like the traditional freedoms encompassed in the Bill of Rights, due process liberty is cordoned off from the intrusive reach of government, it is a far more malleable device—the product of judicial invention and creativity premised on changing customs, fashions, and standards of judgment. The lack of specific grounding in the Constitution encourages flexibility and makes for an ongoing, adaptive process. Yet the absence of a positive basis in the first eight amendments invites a pattern of drift and negativism as readily as one that leads to constructive results. Perhaps uncertainty is the price of discovery and change. But surmise concerning the outcome of litigation at times may prove to be dismaying as well as heartening, as variable, shifting, and unpredictable as are the mores reflected in the opinions of courts generally.

This chapter relates only peripherally to the familiar injunctions founded in the Bill of Rights. The latter still reflects its origins, dating at least from the Age of Enlightenment, though significant glosses building upon its stark provisions have appeared during the past two centuries. Notwithstanding the vibrancy and remarkable cogency of the Bill of Rights, it is due process liberty that is at the center of current controversy. In a myriad of ways, differences revolve as much about the philosophy of Supreme Court appointees as about evolving judicial doctrines that have been crafted to reflect their political or policy preconceptions. Much of the debate over activism and restraint or interpretivism versus noninterpretivism centers about the meanings assigned to due process liberty.

Liberty applications, proposed and actual, have assumed a forward momentum in recent decades. The Fourteenth Amendment's Due Process Clause has served as a significant source of protection against state actions affecting intimate and fundamental personal decisions. From parental control of the education of their children to reproductive options and the structure of familial units, a right to be "let alone" and to be unimpeded by an advancing state-sponsored paternalism has come to the fore. Respect for individual autonomy reached its zenith immediately following the end of the Warren era and, for the most part, it has been safeguarded from overt political intrusion by reference to amorphous liberty interests. It is only when carried to fatuous extremes, unrelated to bona fide safety needs, that courts have been reluctant to intervene. Former Supreme Court Justice Lewis Powell, sitting by designation on circuit, put the issue in perspective when he rejected a plea to hold unconstitutional a state law requiring motorcyclists to wear protective headgear: "[T]he unconstrained right asserted . . . has no discernible bounds, and bears little resemblance to the important but limited privacy rights recognized by our highest Court."[1]

How, then, did due process liberty attain the status of a constitutional imperative, albeit one not always endorsed in full measure either by those on the Court or in political fora? The beginnings were not auspicious when, early in the twentieth century, theories of Social Darwinism—projecting extremist principles of economic laissez-faire—became a part of Fourteenth Amendment case law. A particularly odious precedent, one that has never wholly disappeared from hostile critiques, lay in the much-berated ruling in *Lochner v. New York*.[2] Judicial dogma expounding a liberty of contract in employer-employee relations emerged triumphant, inaugurating a period of unrelenting negativism that, with few exceptions, continued until the late 1930s. The reach of the police power was substantially restricted; liberty took on the outward guise of individual freedom of action when, in fact, it served as a protective shield of private enterprise.

If something more than invasions of economic rights, narrowly construed, was to be deterred, liberty had to be afforded a more expansive scope even in an age of unrequited negativism. That this came to pass in the midst of a wave of xenophobia following World War I is a tribute to the endurance of liberty as an abiding American faith and ideal regardless of passing, aberrant episodes. State restrictions on the teaching of foreign languages to elementary school children were set aside as violative of privileges recognized as "essential to the orderly pursuit of happiness by free men."[3] Subsequently, liberty interests were cited to invalidate a state law that required children between specified ages to attend the public schools, which effectively had thus prevented parents from sending their offspring to private institutions. In unequivocal terms, the Court declared that a child "is not the mere creature of the State."[4]

Though untoward departures occurred, reflective of the then prevailing euphoria over the virtues of sterilization of the mentally ill and convicted felons (particularly during the late 1920s),[5] liberty advances continued to proliferate preceding and during the Warren Court era. The emphasis shifted to family, marriage, procreation, and heterosexual relations generally. Yet fears of expanded perceptions of liberty that might be linked in any way to a real or presumed reversion to *Lochner*, however remote, almost immobilized a Court that had suffered institutional reverses two decades earlier. A possible revival of substantive due process loomed as symptomatic of trauma so acute and forbidding as to be hardly worth the effort.

It was in this light that Justice Douglas, writing for the Court in *Griswold v. Connecticut*,[6] sought a serviceable alternative on which to hold unconstitutional a state's anti-contraception law that had been before the Court on alternative grounds at least twice.[7] He finally settled upon a unique if incredulous formula that led to a contrived combination of constitutional derivatives which, in his estimation, produced "zones of privacy." The sources lay in "penumbras," formed by emanations from no less than five of the first ten amendments. Justice Harlan, concurring, would have proceeded directly by way of the due process clause and a finding that the law violated basic values "implicit in the concept of ordered liberty."[8] To Justice Black, joined by Justice Stewart, however, the Court's findings were little more than a poorly disguised revitalization of principles of "natural justice," a due process concept "no less dangerous when used to enforce this Court's views about personal rights than those about economic rights."[9]

A host of thematic variations, predicated on due process liberty, continued to thrive and to grow notwithstanding Justice Black's misgivings. In a succeeding contraception case,[10] the Court went on to elaborate upon a right of privacy and to sustain an individual's right to be free from "unwarranted governmental intrusion" in deciding on whether to beget or to bear a child. The culmination of these judicial forays occurred in 1973 when, in *Roe v. Wade*[11] and associated abortion rights cases, a majority asserted the right of a woman to decide whether or not to terminate her pregnancy. Justice Blackmun, who prepared the opinion in what proved to be one of the most controversial cases of the decade if not of the post-1973 epoch, apparently felt less constrained to reembrace substantive due process than in the days when Justices Black and Douglas persistently railed against Fifth or Fourteenth Amendment imperatives said to be akin to those in *Lochner* and its progeny. Despite passing references to *Griswold*, the Court took as its predicate the concept of personal liberty. The state's power to protect the health of women was recognized while the notion that life begins at conception was not conceded. Justice Blackmun's references to the trimesters of pregnancy in defining the role of the state re-echoed the familiar soundings of substantive due process—more in the nature of legislative findings and an exercise in obstetrics than the fashioning of a judicial opinion.

Among the most outspoken critics of *Roe v. Wade* was Justice Rehnquist who, in a dissenting opinion, expressed doubt that the right to an abortion was "fundamental." He argued that the Court was moving into perilous terrain, requiring an examination of legislative policies and prompting inquiries into the wisdom of these policies.[12] Even more pointedly, Justice White, dissenting with Rehnquist, condemned the Court's "exercise of raw power" as "improvident and extravagant." He counseled that such issues be left to the people for resolution through the political process. Thus, although the Court divided seven to two, the minority provided significant clues to divisive questions that eventually encompassed the nation.[13] Whether the reach of judicial review could or should extend to issues like abortion recalled heated debates over substantive due process and questions of propriety and desirability that remained conjectural then as they are now.

The vitality of *Roe v. Wade* as an operative precedent has been in doubt since the inception of the Rehnquist Court, arguably even earlier. If it may be assumed that public opinion and legislative decision making play any role in shaping the attitudes of the Justices, surely the abortion rights controversy has been among the most volatile current instances of polemical discourse. Chief Justice Rehnquist and Justices Scalia and White have been implacable foes of the version of substantive due process advanced here. The three have been unrelenting in pursuing a majoritarian approach to the resolution of the prolonged public argument that has engrossed the nation. Justice Scalia, in particular, has been vehement in urging that *Roe v. Wade* be overruled explicitly and without delay. The sole moderating voice among those in the antiabortion rights bloc has been that of Justice O'Connor who, despite her acknowledged opposition to the substance of *Roe v. Wade*, has voted to prevent its total abandonment.

A woman's constitutional right to have an abortion, as set out by Justice Blackmun in 1973, came closest to outright renunciation in the 1989 decision, *Webster v. Reproductive Health Services*.[14] Chief Justice Rehnquist's plurality opinion markedly narrowed the reach of *Roe* and its progeny, but it left the shell of the case "undisturbed" since, according to the line of reasoning followed, there was "no occasion to revisit the holding." Justice O'Connor, concurring, took the plurality to task for proceeding beyond what was necessary to decide the question posed. She declined to accept the state's invitation to reexamine *Roe*; instead, she elected to adhere to basic principles of stare decisis. Justice O'Connor found no need to weigh the constitutional question since it was inessential under the circumstances of the case. If and when the occasion presented itself, she concluded, a reexamination of *Roe v. Wade* should be undertaken with adequate time and care.

Justice Scalia's concurring opinion in *Webster* reiterated at some length his reasons for advocating a direct and explicit overruling of *Roe v. Wade*. He took the Court to task for what he termed its "newly contracted abstemiousness," and he added a particular note of derision for what he took to be Justice O'Connor's "finessing *Roe*." Justice Scalia noted popular and other pressures for the Court to move beyond this "most stingy possible holding." In emphatic language, he chastised the plurality for its irresponsible course and for another in a progression of "indecisive" actions in preserving a "chaos" evident to all "who can read and count."[15]

In a scathing dissent, Justice Blackmun, joined by Justices Brennan and Marshall, assailed the plurality for its deception and for its attempts to "engineer a dramatic retrenchment in our jurisprudence." He defended the framework of *Roe* as one consistent with a constitutional right of privacy protected as a form of liberty under the Due Process Clause. As the author of the prevailing opinion in *Roe v. Wade*, Justice Blackmun berated the plurality for its proposed "revolutionary" revision of abortion law and for inviting "charges of cowardice and illegitimacy." He characterized some of the reasoning as "unadulterated nonsense" while expressing serious misgivings over the future of *Roe* as a viable precedent.

Late in the spring of 1991, the debate over *Roe* resumed within the context of a challenge to the constitutionality of a regulation forbidding clinics and other agencies assisted by federal funds from providing any information, much less counseling, concerning the abortion alternative. Chief Justice Rehnquist, writing for a majority in *Rust v. Sullivan*,[16] sustained the validity of the regulation, but with a surprisingly positive reminder that the right of abortion remained intact. All the same, he argued, government was not obligated to support with tax monies the implementation of or access to that which might facilitate a woman's realization of an acknowledged constitutional right.

Apart from what was perhaps Justice Blackmun's most relentless attack on the Court's antiabortion bloc, two new developments came to light in *Rust v. Sullivan*. Justice O'Connor, joining the dissenters, moved more decisively than in the past toward a midway position on the abortion question. And, without comment, Justice Souter revealed glimpses of antiabortion predilections although his vote, without more, did not prejudge the outcome on the merits. Should significant issues of stare decisis arise and critical political and social issues appear within the confining parameters of judicial colloquy, neither the results nor the course of reasoning pursued may be as readily predictable as politicized advocates anticipate.

If, in *Rust v. Sullivan*, the Court avoided any reference to liberty interests derived from *Roe*, it remained confounding why the majority felt compelled to consider constitutional questions that need not have been reached. The admitted ambiguity of the statute and the questionable nature of the implementing regulations might have resulted in a negative decision, but one striking a note of restive neutrality in a troubled area where the abortion issue lay just beneath a barely obscured veneer. Justices O'Connor and Stevens, in dissent, opted for such a ruling premised on statutory grounds, reserving to Congress the "power to force the constitutional question." The majority's haste in moving to weigh primary sources of authority prompted Justice Blackmun's characterization of the regulations as "viewpoint-based supression of speech" and, in their ultimate reach, as a denial to women of the "ability voluntarily to decide their procreative destiny."[17] As Justice Blackmun viewed the effects of the majority's ruling, the loss of freedom to choose was as destructive for those concerned as an outright ban.

When, in *Planned Parenthood of Southeastern Pennsylvania v. Casey*,[18] state restrictions on abortion rights once again came before the Court for review, much of the state legislation was sustained. But a newly formed coalition, consisting of Justices O'Connor, Kennedy, and Souter, reaffirmed the essential holding of *Roe v. Wade*. The joint opinion, in what can only be described as a novel departure, stressed principles of institutional integrity and the rule of stare decisis and went on to provide an expansive explication of notions of individual liberty. By direct reference to the basic decision in *Roe*, the joint opinion concluded that the 1973 precedent was based on a "constitutional analysis which we cannot now repudiate."[19] Justice Blackmun termed the joint opinion "an act of personal courage and constitutional principle."[20] In a separate opinion, Justice Stevens averred that the Court's holding, in rejecting a "right to life" of the developing fetus, had reiterated a "fundamental premise of our constitutional law governing reproductive autonomy."[21]

Apart from the abortion rights imbroglio (in many respects sui generis), prospects for an extension of due process liberty appeared bleak. When, in 1986, the Court announced a disinclination to sanction any privacy protection for homosexual sodomy, a majority went on to indicate a marked reluctance to take a "more expansive view" of the identification of new fundamental rights grounded in due process. Justice White, who wrote the prevailing opinion in *Bowers v. Hardwick*,[22] pointed out that the Court was "most vulnerable and comes nearest to illegitimacy when it deals with judge-made constitutional law having little or no cognizable roots in the language or design of the Constitution." He maintained that substantive due process had been repudiated in the wake of the prolonged conflict between the judicial and executive branches in the 1930s. The inference was clear that no comparable forays premised on the Fifth and Fourteenth Amendment were contemplated.

More generally, *Bowers* provided the occasion for a broad exchange of views providing insights into the differing philosophies and modes of analysis being advanced. Justice Blackmun, joined in dissent by Justices Brennan, Marshall, and Stevens, dealt at length with the constitutional right to privacy and its implications. His opinion took as its predicate Justice Brandeis' assertion of a "right to be let alone"[23] as the basis for according individuals freedom to choose how to conduct their lives and for assuring the centrality of such rights. Justice Blackmun stressed the scope of the liberty interests at stake—interests of a significantly higher order than those assumed in the majority opinion. To like effect, Justice Stevens, dissenting separately, placed renewed emphasis on the protection extended to "intimate choices" by all persons, married and unmarried, and the intolerability of any intrusions on the "abiding interest" in individual liberty.[24]

The Court returned to its troubled discourse over liberty interests and their scope in 1989 when, in *DeShaney v. Winnebago County Dept. of Social Services*,[25] it examined claims of an affirmative right to governmental assistance that was said to flow from due process liberty. The factual context was a poignant one, involving the physical abuse of a child by his father without intervention by the county social services department when, in fact, a caseworker had become aware of and had recorded such incidents in her files. In a civil rights action, the mother and child charged a due process violation, in effect that the state had failed to provide protective services.

Chief Justice Rehnquist, writing for the majority in *De Shaney*, rejected the notion that the state's failure to act constituted a privation of due process liberty. He acknowledged that substantive due process transgressions might have occurred when incarcerated prisoners and involuntarily committed mental patients had not been properly treated and protected. But affirmative state duties were obligatory only in relation to persons who were not free to act on their own behalf. It was a loss of individual freedom, actuated by state action, that brought into play due process protections linked to a deprivation of liberty.[26] Apart from such limited intrusions, Justice Rehnquist asserted, the Due Process Clause protects people from the state and abuses of power. It was never intended to require the state to shield individuals from mistreatment or assaults inflicted upon one another.

Justice Brennan, joined in dissent by Justices Marshall and Blackmun, denied that the Court was being asked to declare that, in general, constitutional safeguards extended to positive as well as negative liberties. The state had interjected itself, at least in part, accepting some responsibility for the welfare of this child and others in like circumstances. Inaction, then, was as abusive of power as action where, as here, a vital duty was being ignored.[27] Justice Blackmun, dissenting separately, objected to the Court's retreat into a "sterile formalism," drawing rigid lines of separation between action and inaction. Such formalism, Blackmun averred, was contrary to the breadth intended by those who had devised the Fourteenth Amendment.[28]

The amorphous nature of due process liberty was reemphasized in *Michael H. & Victoria D. v. Gerald D.*,[29] a case that offered a blend of complex and wryly amusing elements within a peculiar factual context. The putative father, Michael H., sought paternity rights denied by the California courts on the basis of a statutory presumption that legitimized a child born as the issue of a married couple even if tests appeared to establish the contrary. The probability was great that the child, Victoria D., was the product of an adulterous relationship and that, in fact, the biological father was not the husband. Counter to the presumption, Michael H. asserted a liberty interest in a protected relationship existing between himself as the natural father and the child. The Supreme Court denied Michael H.'s claims and sustained the judgment of the California courts.

Justice Scalia, writing the plurality opinion, elected to undertake an analysis linked to substantive not procedural due process. Initially, he denied that the doctrine of irrebuttable presumptions applied since, if it had, the state's statutory scheme would have been subject to individualized challenges. Justice Scalia took as his basis for denominating an interest as a phase of "liberty" not only that it be "fundamental" but also that it be a traditional interest rooted in the history and conscience of the American people. The purpose of such a rigorous standard, Justice Scalia declared, was to prevent future generations from casting aside significant accepted values, "not to enable this Court to invent new ones."[30] In a controversial footnote, he went on to consult the "most specific tradition available" to establish a rule that creates a binding link to the constitutional text and the identifiable conventions associated with it.[31] Scalia declined to embrace a precept of liberty that, in effect, went beyond safeguarding the unitary family and afforded constitutional protection to parentage on the part of an adulterous natural father.

Justice O'Connor, in a concurring opinion joined by Justice Kennedy, took exception to the mode of historical analysis pursued by the plurality in the footnote cited. She declined to preclude the unanticipated by reference to the unremitting, "single mode" of analysis projected by Justice Scalia.[32] Justice Stevens' concurrence was narrowly conceived, but he left open the possibility that a protected relationship might develop in "unconventional settings." Unlike the plurality, Stevens refused to reject the notion that a natural father might have constitutional interests in a comparable setting.[33]

Justice Brennan, joined in dissent by Justices Blackmun and Marshall, dealt at length with Justice Scalia's confining methodology and its impact on liberty interests. He objected to the plurality's "constitutional universe," said to have placed discernible boundaries about a tradition which, he averred, can be as "malleable and as elusive as liberty itself." Justice Brennan reminded his colleagues that "we are not an assimilative, homogenous society, but a facilitative, pluralistic one" promoting tolerance and a receptivity to the idiosyncrasies peculiar to a diverse populace. An expansive concept of liberty was essential, he stressed, to ensure that the Constitution remained a "living charter," not a "stagnant, archaic, hidebound document steeped in the prejudices and superstitions of a time long past."[34] Justice White, like Justice Brennan, concluded that Michael H. possessed an assured liberty interest. Like Brennan,

White urged that procedural guarantees be observed to afford the putative father an opportunity to establish his paternity.[35]

If, then, due process liberty emerged from the post-*Bowers* cases unimpaired in historical terms but committed to a dormant if not moribund state, little, if any, incremental growth seemed likely for the foreseeable future. The recourse to tradition, narrowly defined and structured, meant that long-held guidelines of constitutional relativism and adaptability to contemporary conditions were being rendered suspect in a Court assiduously dedicated to the past. Yet, as Justice Brennan noted in *Michael H.*, only one additional member of the Court fully endorsed Justice Scalia's approaches to the analysis of questions arising under the Due Process Clause.[36] To assume that a majority had adhered to such a narrow reading of the Constitution is misleading; indeed, it hardly reflects a tribunal long known for its espousal of a spirited version of judicial review.

Apart from peripheral references,[37] liberty interests were reevaluated at length in *Cruzan v. Director, Missouri Department of Health*,[38] a "right-to-die" case that few observers considered likely to be reviewed in the Supreme Court. Such cases had been dealt with in the state courts and, predictably, the difficult issues raised had become primarily matters of state constitutional law rather than ones ascribable to the Fourteenth Amendment. In *Cruzan*, the Supreme Court sustained the judgment of the state court, affirming a "clear and convincing evidence" test to determine the patient's wishes regarding withdrawal of life-prolonging procedures. In doing so, it rejected the "substituted judgment" of close family members that the patient, their daughter, would have preferred not to continue life in a persistent vegetative state.

Chief Justice Rehnquist, who wrote for the Court in *Cruzan*, denied that the Constitution forbade establishment of the procedural safeguards set out by the state. The analytical route selected for exploration, he explained by way of a footnote, was not to be a generalized constitutional right of privacy. Instead, Rehnquist elected to proceed in terms of Fourteenth Amendment liberty interests. There was no question that a competent person had a protected liberty interest in declining to submit to unwanted medical treatment. The preservation of bodily integrity required that informed consent be secured before treatment might be undertaken. Yet, the Court noted, the liberty interest must be balanced against relevant state interests.[39]

When, as here, the alternatives lay between life and death, the state might opt in favor of safeguarding the life of an incompetent person verily unable to make an informed and voluntary choice. The Chief Justice denied that the state need make judgments about the "quality of life" in individualized cases.[40] Nor was the state precluded by protected individual interests from guarding against possible abuses by surrogates whose objectives may not be wholly disinterested and whose views may not be irrefutably those of the patient. Consequently, Justice Rehnquist argued, the state was entitled to impose "heightened" evidentiary requirements evidenced by its recourse to a "clear and convincing" standard.[41] Family decision making, described and acknowledged in traditional terms in *Michael H.*, could not be "turned around" to afford unqualified primacy to close family members where "substituted judgment" must be exercised.[42]

Justice O'Connor, concurring in *Cruzan*, stressed that any forced treatment of an individual implicated significant liberty concerns. These plainly would prevail should a competent adult be faced with the degree of intrusion and restraint necessary to provide nutrition and hydration by artificial means. Aside from *Cruzan*, Justice O'Connor emphasized, the Court's ruling did not foreclose the possibility of a subsequent determination requiring the states to implement the decision of a duly appointed surrogate. The states, in the final analysis, continued to serve as discrete laboratories in crafting appropriate procedures designed to protect the liberty interests of incompetents.[43]

In a second concurring opinion, Justice Scalia charged that the Court was intruding itself unnecessarily into the right-to-die debate that had long engaged the attention of the states. He called upon his colleagues to announce forthrightly that the federal courts had no role to play in this field and that, as before, the states be permitted to proceed without needless federal intervention. Justice Scalia asserted that the Constitution had "nothing to say" about the subject. He admonished the Court to avoid injecting itself into every area of human activity "where irrationality and oppression may theoretically occur, and if it tries to do so it will destroy itself."[44]

Justice Brennan, joined by Justices Marshall and Blackmun, approached the thorny issues posed by *Cruzan* from a distinctly different perspective. Unlike the Court, he took the state's rigorous invocation of a clear and convincing evidence test in a case of this nature as violative of the Due Process Clause. The patient, Justice Brennan protested, is "entitled to choose to die with dignity." Constitutionally protected liberty interests assure her a "fundamental right" to be free of artificial and unwanted nutrition and hydration. And, he added, that right is not outweighed by any compelling state interests asserted in this case. Medical self-determination thus emerged paramount and, although concededly not absolute, it surely had to prevail in the circumstances of the case. Justice Brennan would have held the state's rule of decision unconstitutional because of the significant precepts of liberty at stake here.[45]

Justice Stevens, dissenting separately, stressed the individual's "vital interest in liberty" as a supervening consideration in this case. Like Brennan, Stevens emphasized the liberty interests involved and the unusual necessity of maintaining them inviolate to ensure the proper treatment of seriously ill patients who seek an end of medication and extraordinary or heroic measures of treatment. He took the state's regulation to be an "unreasonable intrusion" upon private matters encompassed within the scope of protected liberty preserved from invasion by the Fourteenth Amendment.[46] Justice Stevens criticized the state's efforts to arrogate to itself the "power to define life" and the Court's indulgence in permitting "this usurpation," thereby placing the patient's life and liberty in "disquieting conflict."[47]

Why, it may be asked, had the majority in *Cruzan* decided to posit a holding linked to definitions of liberty admittedly truncated, rather than to a generalized right of privacy? The latter, it is often said, finds no firm grounding in the Constitution. In *Griswold v. Connecticut*,[48] still among the most controversial cases of the past several decades, Justice Douglas had discovered no explicit textual source. Instead, he had premised privacy values on a congeries of penumbras and emanations attributable to five of the first ten amendments. That a right to privacy, so flimsily supported, has proved to be unsatisfactory doctrinally and unwieldy in its breadth and applications need hardly be explored. It was Justice Harlan who, in *Griswold*, fashioned a right of privacy founded on notions of due process liberty under the Fourteenth Amendment with references to traditional values predicated on a "concept of ordered liberty."

Chief Justice Rehnquist's explanation in *Cruzan* roughly followed the analytical guidelines set out by Justice Harlan. Liberty, it seemed, evinced stronger historic roots with less volatile overtones than a resort to the essentially unconstrained terrain associated with a right to privacy. As in *Michael H.* and *DeShaney*, there were fewer temptations for the Justices to venture beyond the traditionally negative construction of rights and interests cordoned off from governmental intrusion. Liberty, in a sense, offered the potential for virtual stagnation in constitutional development or for a gradualism so excessive as to project few deviations of substance. Why, in fact, the Court elected to review *Cruzan* still remains a mystery, unless there was an intentional linkage to the abortion cases with oblique references to the sanctity of life and its preservation. In any event, it remains doubtful that additional right-to-life cases will reappear in the Supreme Court for some time.

Will liberty interests long be consigned to the inert state anticipated in these cases? It is doubtful, albeit based on separate opinions, that the future will be so bare of meaningful precedents. The Court does not function in a vacuum. The dynamics of American society make it difficult, if not impossible, for the Justices to defer so markedly and abjectly to the state courts or to national legislation or regulations. Liberty is a remarkably flexible concept promotive of growth patterns almost oblivious to the announced predilections of the Court—even one conservative in its tenor and outlook. The presumed commitment to a strict adherence to stare decisis and narrow conceptions of history are too self-limiting to survive over the long term when weighed against the compelling forces of pluralism in a constitutional system marked by recurrent indicators of persistent change.

NOTES

1. Picou v. Gillum, 874 F. 2d 1519 (11th Cir. 1989).
2. 198 U.S. 45 (1905).
3. Meyer v. Nebraska, 262 U.S. 390, 399 (1923).
4. Pierce v. Society of Sisters, 268 U.S. 510, 535 (1925).
5. The most egregious example of "inverse" substantive due process still may be found in Justice Holmes' perverse arguments in Buck v. Bell, 274 U.S. 200 (1927). An incomplete rejoinder and partial refutation on equal protection grounds appeared 15 years later in Skinner v. Oklahoma, 316 U.S. 535 (1942).
6. 381 U.S. 479 (1965).
7. See Tileston v. Ullman, 318 U.S. 44 (1943) and Poe v. Ullman, 367 U.S. 497 (1961).
8. Palko v. Connecticut, 302 U.S. 319 (1937).
9. 381 U.S. at 479 (1965).
10. Eisenstadt v. Baird, 405 U.S. 438 (1972).
11. 410 U.S. 113 (1973).
12. Id. at 173–74.
13. Doe v. Bolton, 410 U.S. 179, 222 (1973). A continuing erosion of abortion rights, without an outright reversal of Roe v. Wade, occurred in a number of cases. See, e.g., Planned Parenthood Ass'n of Kansas City v. Ashcroft, 462 U.S. 476 (1983).
14. 492 U.S. 490 (1989).
15. Id. at 532–37.
16. 114 L. Ed. 2d 233 (1991).
17. Id. at 265, 271.
18. 120 L. Ed. 2d 674 (1992).
19. Id. at 707.
20. Id. at 745.
21. Id. at 739.
22. 478 U.S. 186 (1986).
23. See Olmstead v. United States, 277 U.S. 438 (1928) (dissenting opinion).
24. 478 U.S. at 214–20 (1986).
25. 489 U.S. 189 (1989).
26. See Estelle v. Gamble, 429 U.S. 97 (1976) and Youngberg v. Romeo, 457 U.S. 307 (1982).
27. 489 U.S. at 212.
28. Id. at 212–13.
29. 491 U.S. 110 (1989).
30. Id. at 122 n.2.
31. Id. at 127 n.6.
32. Id. at 132.
33. Id. at 133–36.
34. Id. at 137–57.
35. Id. at 157–63.

36. *Id.* at 136.
37. *See, e.g.*, Washington v. Harper, 494 U.S. 210 (1990), relating to the involuntary administration of antipsychotic drugs to prisoners.
38. 479 U.S. 261 (1990).
39. *Id.* at 278–79.
40. *Id.* at 282.
41. *Id.* at 284.
42. *Id.* at 285–87.
43. *Id.* at 287–92.
44. *Id.* at 292–301.
45. *Id.* at 301–30.
46. *Id.* at 339–51.
47. *Id.* at 351.
48. 381 U.S. 479 (1965).

3

Expressive Conduct and the Means of Communication

DEVELOPMENTAL BENCHMARKS: A SELECTIVE MISCELLANY

The provisions of the First Amendment, long extolled as reflective of the nation's libertarian heritage, have prompted considerable controversy among contemporary commentators regarding the meanings intended. Notions of a basic freedom to dissent have been widely accepted in theory, but erstwhile fears of the effects of "bad sentiments" or "pernicious tendencies" continue to circulate whenever peace and good order are threatened. While the seventeenth-century English law of treason and sedition has passed into history, remnants reappear, albeit transiently, during periods of crisis. Americans readily concur in the Blackstonian formula that condemns previous restraints upon publications. All the same, a consensus is more difficult to attain in assuring freedom from censure for matters when published or otherwise set out. If, in fact, the common law has been superseded by constitutional guarantees developed over two centuries, occasional "backsliding" serves as a reminder that restatements of the law as it existed in the late eighteenth century are not entirely bygone relics of a distant past.

Congressional passage of the Sedition Act of 1798 gave rise to heated debates over the design and purposes of the First Amendment. The imposition of criminal penalties and repeated references to a much-berated law of seditious libel led to political contests that revived old disagreements and contributed to widespread rancor. Expiration of the sedition act and the election of 1800 brought the incident to a temporary close, but animosities endured. No definitive precedents persisted, in part because of apprehension that discouraged judicial challenges lest they result in baneful decisions more detrimental to free expression than the statute itself. To like effect, presidential excesses during the Civil War had little lasting impact. A postwar pronouncement held invalid the trial of civilians before military commissions, attesting to judicial disapproval of procedures menacing individual rights.[1]

It remained for the tumultuous events of the years during and immediately following World War I to give rise to precedents productive of modern doctrines of free expression. Enactment of an espionage act in 1917, followed by adoption of a sedition amendment the following year, led to a series of Supreme Court decisions describing guidelines distinguishing forbidden and protected speech and weighing societal interests against guaranteed liberties. From the outset, it was clear that a literal application of the First Amendment's language, precluding congressional intervention, would not prevail. One of the formulas that persisted was a "clear and present danger" test,[2] exemplified in a series of Holmes-Brandeis dissents[3] and designed to counter the "bad tendency" test of the 1920s.[4] The latter emphasized intent and probable effect, the presumption being that an act regulatory of speech was constitutional.

A second wave of litigation arose prior to and in the course of the McCarthy era. Fears of communist subversion transformed the clear and present danger test, sustained during World War II, into the less compelling phraseology of grave and probable danger. There was a return to the idiom of "bad tendency" in a major case[5] as First Amendment rights of free speech continued to decline. A

gradual turnabout began to occur in the early 1960s. The denouement of the postwar period of turbulence appeared to have occurred
in the Court's holding in *Albertson v. Subversive Activities Control
Board*,[6] predicated principally on Fifth Amendment grounds.
Though issues of free expression did not always control, glimmers
of the First Amendment came through the judicial overlay.[7] In like
manner and almost in parallel fashion, old-style loyalty-security
cases faded into obscurity and all but disappeared as central features
of judicial review.[8] A repressive era had ended, often without
epilogues discernible in the annals of the Court.

As cases related to loyalty oaths and subversion began to abate,
the Court moved to undermine, at times by indirection, the supportive doctrinal framework. Decision making was often grounded in
findings of invalidity tied to vagueness, uncertainty, and excessive
breadth with occasional allusions to expressive liberties.[9] An oath
required of public employees was set aside by reference to the need
for the state to demonstrate specific intent of those affected to
further the illegal aims of specified organizations. Otherwise, the
majority contended, guilt by association would be condoned contrary to the dictates of the First Amendment.[10] More explicitly
libertarian but still premised, in some measure, on defects of
vagueness, the Court announced in *Keyishian v. Board of Regents*[11]
a commitment to the preservation of academic freedom as a "special concern" of the First Amendment that "does not tolerate laws
that cast a pall of orthodoxy over the classroom." Nor might public
employment be conditioned on the forfeiture of rights which,
Justice Brennan asserted, the Constitution guaranteed and which
government could not curtail directly.

Transitional linkages persisted in the early years of the Burger
Court. So-called "negative" oath provisions, forswearing outlawed
associations and beliefs, were downgraded and, in effect, rewritten
to avoid condemnation for vagueness. The principles set out in
recently decided cases such as *Keyishian* were sustained, albeit
within a limited context.[12] Associational rights took on a newfound
vitality[13] though backward thrusts did occur.[14] New interests in
public employee law began to unfold as attention veered from an
emphasis on loyalty issues to the rights of those who worked in

government agencies to express themselves freely with respect to internal matters.

First Amendment claims, advanced by a teacher who had written to a newspaper criticizing the school board's fiscal management, were upheld in *Pickering v. Board of Education*.[15] The Court adopted a balancing test weighing the interests of the employee as a citizen against promotion of the public services provided. As in *Keyishian*, the doctrine of unconstitutional conditions was invoked to ensure that teachers not be compelled to surrender their First Amendment rights to comment on "matters of public interest." All the same, the force of *Pickering* as a precedent was limited to its public concern component even if remarks abutted on some aspects of this component.

The Court, in *Connick v. Myers*,[16] refused to "constitutionalize" an employee grievance based in large measure on circulation of a questionnaire touching upon internal office affairs. Public import was taken to be minimal as determined by content, form, and context. Instead, maintenance of discipline and morale prevailed as issues of public concern were relegated to a lesser level in a judicial assessment of the conduct in question. As Justice White put it for the majority, the First Amendment does not "require a public office to be run as a roundtable for employee complaints over internal office affairs."[17] Justice Brennan, in dissent, took issue with such a narrow conception of subjects of public concern and the degree of deference accorded the employee's judgment. Fears of dismissal, Brennan went on to note, would unduly deter public employees from making available critical materials concerning the performance of elected officials. Such deterrence, as he viewed it, would ill serve the public information function and the dissemination process envisioned by the First Amendment.

Employee interests subsequently were sustained by reference to the *Pickering-Connick* two-prong test in circumstances that, in some respects, were more provocative than those in either of the earlier cases. An employee in a county constable's office, after hearing of the attempted assassination of the president, had conveyed in disparaging terms her hope that a future assault would succeed. In *Rankin v. McPherson*,[18] a closely divided Court held that the discharge was unwarranted in view of the nature of the remarks and the status of the employee. Justice Marshall, writing for the majority, found that the comment, no matter how inappropriate or controversial, dealt with a matter of public concern. The interest of the agency, as an employer, was never jeopardized since the remark was made in a private conversation with a coworker outside the range of the general public. At no point was the effective functioning of the enterprise threatened, Marshall averred, since there was no interference with regular operations or impairment of internal discipline. What is more, the employee's duties were wholly clerical and any effects upon the constable's law-enforcement activities were negligible. Measured in terms of the two-part test, as he viewed it, the free speech rights of the public employee had to prevail. Justice Powell, casting the "swing" vote in a concurring opinion, insisted that the Court's extensive analysis was not called for in a case involving a private, offhand comment, not detrimental to the agency's mission and so lacking in any potential for disruption as to border "on the fanciful."[19]

Nonetheless, Justice Scalia, joined by Chief Justice Rehnquist and Justices White and O'Connor, decried the majority's effort to uphold the employee's right to make the statement without any penalty attaching, a reprimand or assurances that no repetition would occur. Scalia denied that the remark was speech on a matter of public concern but, even if this were to be conceded, he characterized the comment as lying "near the category of completely unprotected speech" and so beyond the core of the First Amendment's protection. Nor did Justice Scalia countenance the Court's differentiation of policy-making and nonpolicy-making personnel since, he noted, the latter may as readily place working relationships in disarray and undermine public confidence[20] as the former.

It is doubtful whether the precedent established in *Rankin v. McPherson* will long endure in the light of pronounced changes in the Court's membership. A five-to-four division never offers a sound or stable basis for longevity, especially in a field as fragile and volatile as that encompassing public employee rights. Should Justice Scalia's rationale command a majority, First Amendment claims in the workplace will be assessed against decidedly less rigorous criteria. Public employees may well need to look to statutory protection, not a constitutional framework that, with respect to speech as it touches upon internal agency operations, has always been flimsy, if not wholly unreliable.

SPEECH AND FORUM REQUIREMENTS

Apart from expressive conduct within the sequestered inner reaches of public agencies or other private areas, speech situations may require intervention by government should communication between individuals result in disruptive behavior or, perhaps less justifiably, the threat of violence. Speech in a public forum, such as a sidewalk, a street, or a park, enjoys the broadest measure of First Amendment protection[21] though access may be restricted in the public interest when egregious conditions warrant it and less rigorous restraints have been explored and found wanting. Justice John Harlan's notion of "speech plus,"[22] referring generally to such activities as picketing, demonstrations, or other projective forms of expression, have been distinguished from "pure speech." The former has been accorded a lesser measure of protection than speech in its "pristine" form.[23] Demonstrations during the troubled years of the 1960s, many either related to the promotion of civil rights causes or prompted by opposition to American involvement in the Vietnamese conflict, tested the bounds of expressive conduct while effecting a studied reconsideration of the permissiveness that previously had come to prevail.[24]

Public forum analysis came into vogue as a significant decisional tool early in the 1980s and has continued to flourish by way of the Supreme Court's identification of three discrete types of fora.[25] The first continues to be the traditional public forum, consisting typically of public streets and parks. Speakers may be excluded only when such action serves a "compelling state interest and the exclusion is narrowly drawn to achieve that interest." A second category relates to a forum created by government designation as an instrumentality for communication. This "designated open forum" functions under standards comparable to those applicable to a traditional public forum and, like it, any content-based restrictions imposed must be narrowly drawn to bring about a compelling state interest. A university campus falls into this grouping[26] though a public school's internal mail system does not.[27] Thus, the forum by designation characterization fails to provide guaranteed access when the property, though publicly owned, is found to be incompatible with expressive activity. The third category, perhaps the most loosely defined but open to the most restrictive intrusions, concerns the nonpublic forum. As a publicly owned facility, it is not committed to "indiscriminate" expressive activities by the public at large and may be reserved for intended purposes. Yet any regulation of speech must be reasonable and must not represent suppression because of opposition to the speaker's opinion.[28]

Regardless of the forum, viewpoint discrimination is not permissible. The First Amendment is taken to forbid any invasion of protected speech linked to a position, judgment, or opinion expressed. Content and subject matter may be considered to control access to a nonpublic forum. But any regulatory effort affecting speech must be viewpoint-neutral.[29] A reasonableness standard applies and restriction of access must be assessed taking into account the forum's purpose and the surrounding circumstances. Nonetheless, no justification will suffice to save an exclusion based on the "desire to suppress a particular point of view."[30] Disapproval of the speaker's views, it is plain, cannot be made the basis for the state to regulate speech. To do so, the opinions repeatedly state or infer, would be an affront to the First Amendment and encroach upon the values that mark a free and open society.

A misdirected effort to designate an airport's central terminal area, in effect, a "First Amendment Free Zone" was rejected by a unanimous Supreme Court. Justice O'Connor, writing for the Court in *Board of Airport Commissioners of Los Angeles v. Jews for Jesus*,[31] condemned the airport commissioners' explicit attempt to exclude all First Amendment activities from the designated area as "facially unconstitutional under the First Amendment overbreadth doctrine regardless of the proper standard."[32] In doing so, the Court avoided the need to decide whether the airport terminal was a traditional public forum or a public forum by government designation. Since Justice O'Connor found no saving construction of the commissioners' sweeping resolution and no merit in claims of nonairport-related speech, it followed, as she viewed it, that there was no need to engage in forum analysis. Justice White, joined by Chief Justice Rehnquist, concurred, but stressed that a majority did not thereby endorse any implication that the airport was, in fact, a traditional public forum. Nor did White agree that the Court should have postponed the forum question for another day.

In a different context, the forum issue reemerged with additional references to bans on displays of hostile messages and anti-congregation restrictions associated with demonstrations in the vicinity of foreign embassies. Congress had added a "display" clause to the District of Columbia Code prohibiting the display of any sign tending to bring the foreign government into "public odium" or "public disrepute." The Court, once again speaking through Justice O'Connor in *Boos v. Barry*,[33] held the clause unconstitutional as a content-based restriction of political speech in a public forum. Even if the protection of the dignity of foreign diplomats might be taken to constitute a "compelling" interest, less restrictive alternatives were found to be available. In this light, Justice O'Connor averred, the display clause was not sufficiently narrowly tailored to survive the exacting scrutiny that the First Amendment required. The display clause was said to operate at the core of the First Amendment since it affected "classically political speech." In addition, Justice O'Connor noted, the clause barred speech in traditional public fora and involved content-based expression. On all counts, then, the section of the code at issue was impermissible affecting, as it did, an entire category of speech.[34]

The Court in *Boos* divided on the "congregation" clause, a majority holding that the text was "problematic" but that a narrowing construction by a federal appeals court had "alleviated" the difficulties. Police authority to disperse congregants, it developed, was not unbridled. Such power could be exercised only when the gathering was directed at the nearby embassy and only when a threat to its security or peace was evident. By virtue of such a narrowing, Justice O'Connor concluded, the congregation clause withstood First Amendment overbreadth review since it did not reach "a substantial amount of constitutionally protected conduct."

The clause merely regulated "the place and manner of certain demonstrations."[35] Justice Brennan, joined by Justice Marshall, entered a separate opinion as did Chief Justice Rehnquist, joined by Justices White and Blackmun. The ends sought and the lines of reasoning followed differed in regard to both clauses as well as the type and the level of scrutiny to be employed conformably to First Amendment needs.

If foreign embassies occupied an ambivalent status in regard to the appropriate variety of forum analysis applicable, a more formidable task obtained when the degree of privacy to be accorded residents of a private home had to be weighed against the picketing protected under the First Amendment. The Court, in *Frisby v. Schultz*,[36] rejected a facial challenge to the ordinance that prohibited picketing before or about individual dwellings. Those picketing, who filed objections to the ordinance, had been engaged in a protest against a physician said to have performed abortions. Justice O'Connor, writing for the Court, found in favor of the privacy interests advanced despite the admitted nature of the town streets as traditional public fora and the stringent First Amendment standards that applied. The ordinance was found to be content neutral, and as the majority viewed it, adequate alternative channels of communication were available for protesters seeking to distribute literature or to disseminate their messages in residential neighborhoods.

What appeared to be determinative of the outcome was the quest for some means of protecting a "captive" audience against the intrusions wrought by objectionable speech. The state had a substantial and justifiable interest, Justice O'Connor declared, in protecting those who are unwilling listeners; the resident was "targeted" and trapped within the confines of the home with "no ready means of avoiding the unwanted speech."[37] It appeared that the obverse side of the First Amendment could be marshalled to shield those who elected not to listen.

The Court's findings in *Frisby*, though persuasive, were not without significant doubts and lingering fears concerning the effects of the restrictive ordinance on First Amendment rights. Additionally, Justice White, concurring, cautioned that applications of the picketing ban had to be narrowly limited to a single residence or the ordinance might be unconstitutional by dint of the overbreadth doctrine. Justices Brennan and Stevens, in separate dissenting opinions, went further in their contentions, stressing that achievement of the residential privacy objective could have been accomplished without so broad an assault on communicative channels. Justice Brennan complained that "substantially more speech than is necessary" might be suppressed.[38] Justice Stevens was apprehensive that town officials had been afforded excessive discretion in the enforcement process.[39]

In a plurality opinion in *United States v. Kokinda*,[40] Justice O'Connor, joined by Chief Justice Rehnquist and Justices Scalia and White, found that a postal "sidewalk" constituted a nonpublic forum with the government acting as proprietor rather than lawmaker. It was said to be a "long-settled principle" that, under the circumstances of the case, governmental actions were liable to be tested by a "lower level" of First Amendment scrutiny. As a result, the regulations imposed were required to meet no more than a "reasonableness" standard. The postal service's "generous accommodation" of some avenues of speech, Justice O'Connor declared, attested to its willingness to provide as broad a forum as possible conformably with its mission. But the service need go no further than permitting the distribution of literature. Efforts to press for the in-person solicitation of funds, the plurality avowed, would be "disruptive" of postal business and would hamper the "normal flow of traffic."[41]

Justice Kennedy, concurring in the judgment in *Kokinda*, seemed more uneasy than was the plurality concerning the forum designation noted. Though he agreed with Justice O'Connor that in-person solicitation of funds could be properly banned to facilitate postal transactions, he opted to apply traditional time, place, and manner guidelines to sustain the agency's regulations. Justice Kennedy sought to avoid any "precise" determination of the status of this postal sidewalk. But he did acknowledge that it was "more than a nonpublic forum."[42]

Justice Brennan's dissent in *Kokinda* took pains to express doubts concerning the use of public forum analysis in this case and elsewhere. He questioned whether the manner in which it was being applied served "to obfuscate rather than clarify" the issues. With respect to the case before the Court, Justice Brennan berated the plurality's insistence "with logic that is both strained and formalistic" that the postal sidewalk was not a public forum. To him this was an unmistakable conclusion that could not be obscured by "doctrinal pigeonholing, [a] complex formula, or [a] multipart test."[43]

If, as seems clear from the Court's opinion in *Frisby*, a private home is to be treated as a sanctuary even when it results in arguably untoward restrictions on public issue picketing, questions remain concerning solicitation intended to elicit funds. Charitable solicitation, the Court has repeatedly held, involves protected speech interests within the purview of the First Amendment's shielded reach and ought not to be treated as commercial speech.[44] Yet aspects of the doctrinal framework shift somewhat when the regulatory power of the state is interjected for the professed purpose of preventing fraud and the imposition of excessive fees by professional fundraisers. Does such a resort to state authority have an adverse effect upon the dissemination of ideas, long regarded as an integral part of charitable solicitation? The Court was called upon to consider this issue as it agreed to review a multi-tiered regulatory scheme in *Riley v. National Federation of the Blind of North Carolina*.[45]

Justice Brennan, writing for the Court in *Riley*, approached the statutory formula of economic regulation in traditional fashion with an emphasis on the First Amendment values that had to be unalterably sustained. The professional fundraisers were said to enjoy interests in speech though it was difficult to link regulation of their activities as directly burdensome on the charities' constitutionally guaranteed rights. A majority refused to accept the state's contention that at issue was merely a matter of economic regulation with no substantial First Amendment implications to be tested at a minimal level of rationality. The state's resolve to protect against assumed wrongdoing, Justice Brennan argued, conflicted with the constitutional mandate that any regulation of speech "must be measured in minimums, not maximums."[46] To do otherwise, except for a narrowly tailored regulation not represented here, threatened expressive freedom and the "chill and uncertainty" engendered might drive professional fundraisers out of the state to the detriment of the charities concerned.

In a dissenting opinion, Chief Justice Rehnquist, joined by Justice O'Connor, took pains to decry the majority's attempt to link the constitutional guarantees associated with charitable solicition as such to the fundraisers. The two were not so interrelated, he avowed, as to obliterate the functional differences between them. Therein lay the constitutional distinction, as he saw it, that minimized the burden on protected speech resulting from economic regulation of the fundraisers. On the record presented, then, Chief Justice Rehnquist took exception to the Court's application of a strict scrutiny test under the First Amendment when, in fact, the impact of the statute more accurately should have been characterized as "remote or incidental." No more than a determination of "reasonableness" was said to suffice for a holding in support of a regulatory effort that, in regard to commercial transactions, served compelling state interests.[47]

CONDUCT AS EXPRESSIVE BEHAVIOR AND SYMBOLIC SPEECH

Nonverbal expression has been included within the ambit of First Amendment protection since it first evidenced itself more than half a century ago.[48] Yet the most compelling cases arose during the troubled era of the 1960s when widespread protests were lodged against American involvement in Vietnam, and civil rights groups sought to reverse segregationist practices, notably in the states of the Old Confederacy.[49] One of the most cited of these cases did not represent a victory for expressive freedom but rather a vehicle through which the Warren Court set out a formula that survived and established guidelines for the disposition of succeeding controversies. In *United States v. O'Brien*,[50] Chief Justice Warren suggested a multiple test as the basis for justifying governmental intervention and regulation. Essentially, state or federal action had to further an "important or substantial governmental interest," be within the constitutional power of government, and be unrelated to "suppression" of free expression. If incidental restrictions on First Amendment liberties resulted, they could extend no further than was essential to serve the federal or state interest claimed. All the same, the draft card burning at issue in *O'Brien* was not held to be a constitutionally protected activity.

Symbolic speech emerged unimpaired in *Tinker v. Des Moines School District*[51] where the Court considered the display of anti-Vietnam armbands worn in protest by students in a public school. A majority found the behavior at issue "closely akin to 'pure speech' "—expression that neither intruded upon the "work of the school . . . [nor] . . . the rights of other students." Freedom of expression could not be overcome, Justice Fortas wrote for the majority, by "undifferentiated fear or apprehension of disturbance." It was this type of "hazardous freedom" that was basic to the nation's strength and independence in what he termed "this relatively permissive, often disputatious, society."[52]

Desecration of the national flag has presented issues that touched especially sensitive chords in the development of symbolic speech. Is it possible to sanction flag burning or other misuse as expression protected by the First Amendment or is the act itself properly before the Court for review? Justice Harlan, in *Street v. New York*,[53] avoided the question directly by adverting to the "fighting words" associated with the act as central to the conviction. In response, the dissenters took the Court to task for converting a flag-burning proceeding into an assumed conviction for speech alone. Justice Fortas, in dissent, referred to the flag as a "special kind of personality . . . traditionally and universally subject to special rules and regulations."[54] Justice Black, dissenting, found it immaterial that words had been spoken on the occasion of the act of burning.[55] Recurrently, the most serious point of contention related to the fact that a closely divided Court had focused upon speech in *Street* where the locus of the charge lay elsewhere, that is, in the desecration of the flag. Support for collateral expressive activity under these conditions postponed an ultimate reckoning that had to address the flag issue itself and notions of symbolic speech expressly attached to it.

The Court, in a per curiam opinion, treated the flag issue within an "improper use" framework as it dealt with the attachment of an emblem as a peace symbol. Once again the central question was bypassed in what was said to be a "private" act of protest, placing the flag outside an apartment window to protest the invasion of Cambodia and the Kent State assault. The Court overturned the conviction as a "pointed expression of anguish" about domestic and foreign affairs—the conveyance of an idea through activity.[56] Justice Rehnquist, joined by Chief Justice Burger and Justice White in dissent, described the prevailing opinion as lacking "all substance" and demonstrating a "total misunderstanding of the State's interest in the integrity of the American flag."[57] Symbolic speech, as before, was never defined with precision in relation to an act of flag misuse or desecration.

The perception of conduct as expressive behavior reappeared in two flag desecration cases decided in 1989 and 1990. The first, *Texas v. Johnson*,[58] brought before the Court a flag-burning incident outside the 1984 Republican National Convention in Dallas, Texas, when a malcontent protested policies of the Reagan administration and of certain local corporations. Since the state law did not permit prosecution for the accompanying comments critical of the flag, Johnson's conviction centered about the burning itself, not the utterance of insulting words. The dissident was found guilty of having violated a state law that made it a crime to "intentionally or knowingly" desecrate the flag of the nation or state. From this ruling, Johnson pursued an unsuccessful appeal from the trial court to an intermediate state court. Subsequently, the Texas Court of Criminal Appeals reversed his conviction on traditional First Amendment grounds with findings predicated on accepted views of symbolic speech and the absence of any threats of a serious disturbance of the peace. The state proceeded to the Supreme Court, seeking reinstatement of Johnson's conviction in the trial court.

Justice Brennan, joined by Justices Marshall, Blackmun, Scalia and Kennedy, sustained the holding of the Texas Court of Criminal Appeals. The Supreme Court thereby acquiesced in that court's view that Johnson could not be punished for burning the flag in the circumstances. While Justice Brennan's opinion was an eloquent reaffirmation of principles of expressive freedom, it added little of substance to precedents previously established. If anything, Justice Brennan's arguments were largely responsive to the state's allegations that, it was said, missed the point of the Court's earlier decisions. He reiterated the "bedrock principle" of First Amendment jurisprudence that expression could not be prohibited because it was found to be offensive or disagreeeable. And, in what might have proved to be a ruinous course for the First Amendment, Brennan suggested that no "separate juridical category" existed for the American flag nor did he wish to create for the flag "an exception to the joust of principles protected by the First Amendment."59 It was this notion of a separate category, albeit to the achievement of an end that Justice Brennan would have decried, which dominated the deliberations of those who reacted with profound hostility to the decision. To their way of thinking, the First Amendment required alteration to permit punitive action against persons convicted of flag desecration. Except for congressional opposition, a dilution of the First Amendment might well have become a reality.

To the apparent surprise of many courtwatchers, Justices Scalia and Kennedy, among the most conservative members of the Court, agreed with the majority's findings. Justice Kennedy took pains to note how wrenching his decision had been in his allusions to the "personal toll" exacted, the repugnance of Johnson's statements, and his "distaste" for the result. He also referred to the "costs" involved for the commitment to "that freedom which sustains the human spirit."60

Chief Justice Rehnquist, joined by Justices White and O'Connor, berated the Court for its support of an "inarticulate grunt or roar" (the burning of the flag) not to express an idea but to antagonize others. He also reproved Justice Brennan for his "patronizing civics lecture" and his impartation to the Court of the role of a "platonic guardian" cautioning those accountable to the public as if they were "truant school children."61 Though these warnings attested to the distinctly political coloration of this case, Chief Justice Rehnquist's own peroration was similarly replete with emotional, scarcely relevant reviews of the unique place of the flag in the nation's history.[62] Justice Stevens' dissent, though less emotive in its impact, was equally critical of the Court's actions which, to him, confused disagreeable ideas with disagreeable conduct that diminished the value of an "important national asset."[63]

Congressional enactment of the Flag Protection Act of 1989 as a way of blunting pressures for a constitutional amendment led to a second review of the flag-burning issue. The Supreme Court, dividing five-to-four as before, held the law unconstitutional in *United States v. Eichman.*[64] In its presentation, the Government urged the Justices to hold that flag desecration, much in the manner of "fighting words," was expression not secured by the First Amendment. Justice Brennan, who wrote again for the Court, declined to do so. He admitted that Congress had not included an explicit content-based limitation, but he refused to sanction what he took to be the "suppression of free expression" out of concern for its likely impact. The act, having been subjected to "most exacting scrutiny," fell as violative of the First Amendment despite "Congress' recent recognition of a purported 'national consensus' favoring a prohibition on flag-burning."[65] Justice Stevens, in a dissent joined by Chief Justice Rehnquist and Justices White and O'Connor, referred to his previous objections in *Johnson* as still of "controlling importance." He noted that the Court was doing "nothing more than reconfirming what it [had] already decided."[66]

Why, it may be asked, was the Court not content to stay its hand and to deny review in *Johnson* when a Texas appellate court had held the punitive state law unconstitutional and the offender had been set free? It is difficult to detect any constructive rationale in support of a full-scale judicial foray when the goals sought by a majority had been attained and little of doctrinal significance conceivably could have been added. Perhaps intervention served the state's initial, hoped-for purposes. But restraint was clearly the prudent course in anticipation of the grievous consequences that seemed certain to follow the invalidation of a flag desecration statute. In fact, adoption of a constitutional amendment diminishing the effectiveness of the First Amendment was narrowly averted only because of congressional reluctance to support any measure appreciably weakening the Bill of Rights. Had an attenuation of expressive liberty come to pass, the Court's penchant for activism might well have proved to be a costly and ill-advised venture in judicial overreach.[67]

COMMERCIAL SPEECH AS PROTECTED EXPRESSION

Until the mid-1970s, commercial speech was not accorded any appreciable degree of First Amendment protection—surely not providing levels characteristic of other forms of expression. The state's regulatory power prevailed in relation to what was termed "purely" commercial speech or corporate efforts to influence policy decisions. At most there were scant hints, despite a decidedly negative outcome in a seminal 1942 case,[68] that a lesser measure of protection might one day apply though no substantial restraints on government could be derived from the existing corpus of decisions. A penchant in favor of sustaining the state's power continued to be evident throughout the cases, perhaps a reflection of the Court's post-1937 reluctance to overturn almost any economic regulatory schemes, federal or state. Yet it was becoming increasingly difficult for the Justices to reject cavalierly all traces of expressive guarantees regardless of the source and the message conveyed.

A limited turnabout occurred in 1975 when, in *Bigelow v. Virginia*,[69] the Court upheld as protected speech a newspaper's publication of an advertisement concerning the availability of out-of-state abortions. The victory was not a compelling one in view of the subject matter. But it did exhibit a willingness to consider some form of commercial speech as protected expression, and it prepared the way for subsequent inroads. The following year, in *Virginia Pharmacy Board v. Virginia Consumer Council*,[70] Justice Blackmun commented unreservedly for the Court that with *Bigelow* "the notion of unprotected 'commercial speech' all but passed from the scene." Though Blackmun's statement was exaggerated, it at least signaled the opening of a new era. A majority attested to society's "strong interest in the free flow of commercial information" and affirmed the proposition that speech did not forgo First

Amendment protection because money had been spent to project it.[71] Nonetheless, the Court indicated by way of a footnote that commercial speech was not "wholly undifferentiable" from other forms and that state regulation was permissible in assuring that the "stream of commercial information flows cleanly as well as freely."[72]

During the mid-1970s and 1980s, the Court embarked upon a series of cases relating to advertising by attorneys. In *Bates v. State Bar of Arizona*,[73] a closely divided Court, speaking through Justice Blackmun, supported the general principle that the range of fees charged for legal services might be advertised despite counter-claims of a negative impact on professionalism. A unanimous Court subsequently set aside as unconstitutional a state's restrictions confining advertising by lawyers to specified categories of information.[74] An even bolder effort by attorneys, in their quest for clients, involved the explicit depiction of an intrauterine device that was said to have caused injury to women. The state took exception to such advertising, but the Court, in an opinion by Justice White, rejected intercession on behalf of members of the public who might have found the drawings offensive or embarrassing. White denied that the state's interest sufficed to warrant the suppression of First Amendment rights.[75]

In an ever-broadening expansion of the scope of permissible advertising, the Court declined to sanction a state ban on direct-mail solicitation when attorneys focused upon a specific segment of the population. Justice Brennan rejected the state's defense that such advertising could engulf and perhaps "overwhelm" those thought to require the services offered.[76] Apparently the breadth of the Court's permissiveness here and in the other lawyer advertising cases exceeded what Justice O'Connor took to be the appropriate bounds of propriety. In a dissenting opinion, she cautioned that *Bates* and its progeny had proved to be "problematic" in denying the states their proper regulatory role in this area.[77] Justice O'Connor undertook a reexamination of the analytical framework of what was becoming a long line of lawyer advertising cases which, she averred in retrospect, had been built on "defective premises and flawed reasoning."[78]

In the midst of criticism of increasingly audacious legal advertising measures, a challenge reached the Court linked to a state supreme court's censure of an attorney for his use of letterhead attesting to certification that, it was claimed, might mislead the public.[79] Justice Stevens, in a plurality opinion, denied that the credentials noted were actually or inherently misleading for, he asserted, "we reject the paternalistic assumption that the recipients of petitioner's letterhead are no more discriminating than the audience for children's television."[80] He rejected any notion that the judgment of the state supreme court was insulated from review for constitutional infirmity and once again pointed to the constraints imposed by the First Amendment. Responding to Justice Stevens' unsteady reliance on the commercial speech doctrine, Justice O'Connor decried its "rote application" and the Court's embroilment in the "micromanagement" of the state's authority to police the ethical standards of the legal profession.[81] Like Justice White in a separate dissent, O'Connor pointed to divisions in the Court as indicative of agreement by a majority that the certification claimed was "at least potentially misleading."[82]

If the most recent lawyer advertising cases exemplify the nebulous status of commercial speech in a specific context, the doctrine itself more generally has come to be regarded as occupying an uneasy place in the galaxy of protected First Amendment rights. A rigorous least-restrictive means test no longer applies to commercial speech cases as a majority concluded in *Board of Trustees of the State University of New York v. Fox*.[83] Justice Scalia, speaking for the Court, substantially modified earlier precedents[84] in this regard. He refused to reimpose an excessively heavy burden on the state though he stopped short of espousing the permissiveness characteristic of the rational basis test. Instead, Justice Scalia spoke of a "reasonable fit" between legislative objectives and the means chosen to attain them. The government's goal must be substantial, and the cost needs to be carefully calculated. But, he asserted repeatedly, commercial speech must be looked upon and treated as subordinate in the scale of constitutional values.[85] Apparently the commercial speech doctrine had fallen to such depths in *Fox* that Justice Blackmun, in dissent, expressed a preference for postponing the least-restrictive means question to another day and deciding the case on grounds of overbreadth.[86] That the Court did agree to this lesser predicate is indicative of the precipitous state of the commercial speech doctrine and the poor prospects for its survival in the Rehnquist Court.

FREEDOM OF ASSOCIATION AND EXPRESSIVE RIGHTS

Decisions implicating associational rights traditionally have related to liabilities imposed upon persons exposed to physical and economic retaliatory measures because of their affiliation with other individuals. Several decades ago, the Supreme Court held unconstitutional efforts to compel disclosure of membership lists by a civil rights organization as an undue restraint upon the members' rights to associational freedom.[87] Such rights, the Court has stated, are secured not only against "heavy-handed frontal attack" but also from being repressed by more subtle means.[88] Apart from a civil rights context and even more remote in terms of a litany of major occurrences lay time-honored organizational rights of workers to form unions and to promote views to which they may be committed.[89]

A so-called "striker amendment" to the Food Stamp Act, passed by Congress in 1981, revived questions touching upon the associational rights of union members but in a changed framework. At issue was the validity of a provision preventing the establishment of a household's eligibility to participate in the food stamp program while a member of the household was on strike or increasing the stamps allotted because of decreased income attributable to the strike. Labor unions and individual union members challenged this section of the law, charging that their First Amendment rights had been violated because of interference with the strikers' rights to maintain suitable ties with their families and with other union members. Additionally, it was claimed, expressive rights regarding union matters were being subjected to curtailment by the government's threat of coercion. A series of equal protection complaints revolved about an alleged "animus" said to disadvantage an unpopular group as well as impermissible incursions directed against family members neither initiating nor joining the strike action. In *Lyng v. Automobile Workers*,[90] the Court, speaking through Justice White, sustained the amendment as unlikely to affect adversely existing family arrangements or "directly and substantially" to interfere with such human linkages. At the same time, a majority denied that the rights of union members were being infringed since no exaction of beliefs was required and no associational rights were abridged. Instead, Justice White asserted, Congress had done no more than refuse to subsidize strike actions or to minimize economic hardships attendant upon such actions. The Constitution, he explained, does not require the government to "furnish funds to maximize the exercise of that right."[91] To the equal protection claims, Justice White responded by resorting to a minimal rational basis standard. He went on to note the Court's reluctance to negate legislative perceptions of the "wisdom" of economic and social policy though he admitted that the statute worked "at least some discrimination" against strikers and those in their households.[92] Justice Marshall, joined in dissent by Justices Brennan and Blackmun, condemned the Court's "dismissive approach" to the equal protection issues posed even as he elected to disregard questions of associational freedom under the First Amendment except by way of a brief passing reference in a footnote.[93]

The dissenters' inattention to First Amendment claims in *Lyng* was remarkable even if, as Justice Marshall averred, the equal protection challenge served as the "centerpiece" of the appeal pursued by several labor unions and their members. Why, it may be asked, was there a total absence of consideration of expressive interests that, deftly put, could have been construed as essential denials of the right to unionize or at least to seek remedies necessary for the achievement of common goals by lawful means? It is possible that the effort to avoid treatment of First Amendment interests was purposeful. That an evasive course was followed is understandable not so much for a lack of adequate arguments to sustain the range of associational rights advanced here but because such an exercise, expansively developed, might have disserved egalitarian objectives juxtaposed against libertarian values in other cases where the contrasting interests could not readily be reconciled. Such a compromise, adversely affecting First Amendment rights (an "incidental abridgment"), had previously been effected to guard against gender discrimination, particularly sexual stereotyping, in *Roberts v. United States Jaycees.*[94]

Central to the Rehnquist Court's review of associational rights was the challenge leveled in *Board of Directors of Rotary International v. Rotary Club of Duarte.*[95] At issue were questions that roughly paralleled those presented in the Jaycees case though in the *Rotary* case the Court elaborated at some length on the principles enunciated earlier. It developed that Rotary International had revoked the charter of a California club because it admitted three women contrary to a policy limiting membership to men. Thereupon, the local club instituted suit against the international organization, asserting that the gender restrictions imposed violated the state's civil rights statute guaranteeing equal accommodations. To this charge, the international responded by premising its defense of gender-based exclusion on a freedom of association predicate.

The crux of the dispute, as Justice Powell framed it for the Court in *Rotary Club*, once again lay in what was fast becoming a familiar two-part First Amendment categorization. Following *Roberts*, the Court held that freedom of association could be viewed in distinct senses distinguished as private and expressive association. Private association encompassed fundamental elements of liberty including marriage, the begetting and bearing of children, child rearing and education, cohabitation with family members, and other intimate personal attachments. Such relationships among Rotary Club members, Justice Powell made clear, did not warrant constitutional protection.[96]

It was the second element of the formula, expressive association, to which Powell devoted most intensive scrutiny. As the Court defined this form of association, expressive rights implicated activities touching upon public questions in pursuit of specific political, economic, social, or other ends. No First Amendment interests were unduly transgressed, Justice Powell wrote, since the Rotary Clubs were dedicated primarily to humanitarian service, peace, and goodwill. If the state's civil rights act caused "some slight infringement" of expressive association, it served the state's "compelling interest" in assuring equal access to women. And, Justice Powell made plain, no distinctions had been made on the basis of the organization's viewpoint,[97] the latter striking a chord of considerable sensitivity in traditional First Amendment jurisprudence. That associational rights premised on the First Amendment were not to be permitted to expand limitlessly or to apply in all possible instances became clear in *City of Dallas v. Stanglin*,[98] a case that raised novel questions of social association. A challenge to a city ordinance placing age restrictions (14 to 18) on dance hall patrons advanced claims that such rights had been violated. Chief Justice Rehnquist, writing for the Court, rejected any assumption that a newly asserted, generalized right of social association was protected. Any failed opportunities that teenagers might suffer in not meeting persons outside the prescribed age bracket found no remedy in constitutional terms. The Chief Justice went on to state that the activities sought to be safeguarded involved neither "intimate human relationships" nor expressive association linked to the advocacy of public causes envisioned by the First Amendment. Recreational dancing, facilitating no more than chance encounters among otherwise unattached individuals, did not rise to the level of a new, safeguarded form of association.

Interestingly, Justice Stevens, joined by Justice Blackmun in a concurring opinion in the Dallas case, departed from the Court's reasoning, rejecting not only the First Amendment claims but also the equal protection clause predicates to which Chief Justice Rehnquist had referred by way of a minimal rationality test. To Stevens, the critical issue concerned the liberty phase of substantive due process, not freedom of association under the First Amendment. It was in this context, he concluded, that the ordinance afforded teenagers a "greater opportunity to associate" than they would have had if the provision had been invalidated. Thus the "modest impairment" of the liberty of those in the age group affected was adequately justified within the accepted bounds of the Fourteenth Amendment.[99]

On balance, the current state of expressive freedoms in the Rehnquist Court, though clearly not at the apex of libertarian activism, does not suggest any marked dilution of constitutional values. Negative changes, where they have occurred, generally have been at the periphery rather than at the center of the decisional process. Perhaps the rights of public employees to express themselves diminished, but conditions in the workplace have never equaled those that citizens enjoy in the society at large. Public forum analysis continues to build upon and to develop increasingly finite levels of categorization. There is a tendency to apply lesser measures of scrutiny within factual contexts that previously have been subjected to exacting tests. In sum, a less broadly crafted, but not a critically deficient, framework of expressive liberty emerges as a result of these developments.

Perhaps the most significant alteration of course has occurred in regard to commercial speech. If the doctrinal structure has not been torn asunder, its future growth and even its survival are in jeopardy. That commerical speech never fully attained a status comparable to other phases of expressive conduct has long been evident. Yet it is not apparent that even an intermediate level of scrutiny has taken hold and will serve to shape prospective guidelines. All the same, there is little likelihood that commercial speech formulas will plunge to a plane of mere rationality review that, in effect, will take it beyond the pale of First Amendment protection. While incontrovertibly negative elements control in this area, a compromise is still possible that may restore some, though not all, of the protective mantle that prevailed earlier.

Associational freedoms seem secure in this Court as they have been, at different stages and in different forms, for the past several decades. What has changed is the nature of the reconciliatory effort required in the weighing of equities. Justice Brennan set the stage in the Jaycees case for the essential subordination, however minimal, of private associational rights compelling them to yield to egalitarian considerations, especially those linked to the elimination of gender-based discrimination. To the contrary, little was lost when, in the Dallas dance hall case, the Court declined to extend First Amendment safeguards to vaguely defined and well-nigh indefensible claims of "social association." But retrogression did occur, reflecting an uncharacteristically strong anti-union animus, in *Lyng* where the Court sustained a federal law preventing the initiation of food stamp distribution to families, any of whose members had gone on strike. The act of Congress, and the Court's favorable disposition of its provisions, is reminiscent of earlier years when unions were looked upon as instruments of ferment and of zealous anti-social conduct.

Missing from the Rehnquist Court's roster were issues that characterized much of the Warren Court's agenda. Nowhere was there the repressive conduct of the McCarthy era with which the Court had to contend through the mid-years of the twentieth century. A true test of the current Court's attitudes toward expressive freedom might be gauged from a recurrence of events mirroring this trying period though, fortunately for the nation, such a turn to the extreme Right does not appear to be probable.

What did come through as remarkable, if no more than an aberration, was the majority's reaction to two instances of flag-burning, both at the state and federal levels. Several of the most conservative members of the Court joined the shrinking liberal faction in holding unconstitutional efforts to punish acts of symbolic speech abhorrent to a large segment of American society. First Amendment liberties, it appears, sometimes make for strange alliances—unexpectedly cohesive in the least likely circumstances. Like its predecessors, the Rehnquist Court has revealed departures in this area that are unpredictable and open to greater shifts and modifications than might be expected.

NOTES

1. Ex parte Milligan, 4 Wall. 2 (1866).
2. Schenck v. United States, 249 U.S. 47 (1919).
3. *See also* Justice Brandeis' concurring opinion in Whitney v. California, 274 U.S. 357 (1927).
4. *See, e.g.,* Gitlow v. New York, 268 U.S. 652 (1925).
5. Dennis v. United States, 341 U.S. 494 (1951).
6. 382 U.S. 70 (1965). *See also* United States v. Robel, 389 U.S. 258 (1967).
7. The virtual demise of the clear and present danger test and its less sanguine antecedents may be found in Brandenburg v. Ohio, 395 U.S. 444 (1969).

8. Samplings of early decisions appear in Speiser v. Randall, 357 U.S. 513 (1958) and First Unitarian Church v. Los Angeles, 357 U.S. 545 (1958). For latter-day variations, *see* Spevack v. Klein, 385 U.S. 511 (1967) and Gardner v. Broderick, 392 U.S. 273 (1968).

9. Cramp v. Board of Public Instruction, 368 U.S. 278 (1961); Baggett v. Bullitt, 377 U.S. 360 (1964).

10. Elfbrandt v. Russell, 384 U.S. 11 (1966).

11. 385 U.S. 589 (1967).

12. Cole v. Richardson, 405 U.S. 676 (1972).

13. *See* the public licensing cases, Baird v. State Bar of Arizona, 401 U.S. 1 (1971) and Application of Stolar, 401 U.S. 23 (1971).

14. Law Students Research Council v. Wadmond, 401 U.S. 154 (1971).

15. 391 U.S. 563 (1968).

16. 461 U.S. 138 (1983).

17. *Id.* at 149.

18. 483 U.S. 378 (1987).

19. *Id.* at 393.

20. *Id.* at 395–401.

21. Hague v. C.I.O., 307 U.S. 496 (1939).

22. The phrase is used in NAACP v. Button, 371 U.S. 415 (1963).

23. *See* Cox v. Louisiana, 379 U.S. 536 (1965). Picketing was initially afforded the status of a protected speech interest under the First Amendment in Thornhill v. Alabama, 310 U.S. 88 (1940), but subsequent decisions have been uneven in terms of the degree of protection extended in varying circumstances.

24. The cases were many and varied. *See, e.g.*, Bell v. Maryland, 378 U.S. 226 (1964); Brown v. Louisiana, 383 U.S. 131 (1966); Adderly v. Florida, 385 U.S. 39 (1967).

25. The three types of fora were recognized and distinguished in Perry Education Ass'n. v. Perry Local Educator's Ass'n., 460 U.S. 37 (1983). Additional clarification and modifications of the Court's classifications may be gleaned from opinions (both majority and dissenting ones) in United States Postal Serv. v. Council of Greenburgh Civic Ass'n., 453 U.S. 114 (1981) and Cornelius v. NAACP Legal Defense and Educational Fund, 473 U.S. 788 (1985).

26. Widmar v. Vincent, 454 U.S. 263 (1981).

27. 460 U.S. at 45.

28. Justice O'Connor, writing for the Court in *Cornelius*, 473 U.S. at 811, made clear that the "existence of reasonable grounds for limiting access to a nonpublic forum . . . will not save a regulation that is in reality a facade for viewpoint-based discrimination."

29. 460 U.S. at 49.

30. 473 U.S. at 812.

31. 482 U.S. 569 (1987).

32. 482 U.S. at 573.

33. 485 U.S. 312 (1988).

34. *Id.* at 318–29.

35. *Id.* at 329–32.
36. 487 U.S. 474 (1988).
37. *Id.* at 487.
38. *Id.* at 496.
39. *Id.* at 499.
40. 479 U.S. 720 (1990).
41. *Id.* at 733–36.
42. *Id.* at 737–39.
43. *Id.* at 741–43.
44. Schaumburg v. Citizens for a Better Environment, 444 U.S. 620 (1980); Maryland v. Munson Co., 467 U.S. 947 (1984).
45. 487 U.S. 781 (1988).
46. *Id.* at 790.
47. *Id.* at 808–13.
48. *See, e.g.*, Stromberg v. California, 283 U.S. 359 (1931).
49. Within a civil rights context, protest by "silent and reproachful presence" in a regional public library was sustained in Brown v. Louisiana, 383 U.S. 131 (1966). *Cf.* the jailhouse demonstration case, Adderley v. Florida, 385 U.S. 39 (1966).
50. 391 U.S. 367 (1968).
51. 393 U.S. 503 (1969).
52. *Id.* at 505–9.
53. 394 U.S. 576 (1969).
54. *Id.* at 616.
55. *Id.* at 609–10.
56. Spence v. Washington, 418 U.S. 405 (1974).
57. *Id.* at 418, 420.
58. 491 U.S. 397 (1989).
59. *Id.* at 414–18.
60. *Id.* at 420–21.
61. *Id.* at 432–35.
62. *Id.* at 421–28.
63. *Id.* at 438–39.
64. 496 U.S. 310 (1990).
65. *Id.* at 318.
66. *Id.* at 323–24.
67. For a brief critique of this episode, see Stanley H. Friedelbaum, *Marginal Notes on Flag Desecration: The Supreme Court, Congress, and the State Courts,* I St. Const. *Commentaries and Notes,* 24–27 (Summer, 1990).
68. Valentine v. Chrestensen, 316 U.S. 52 (1942).
69. 421 U.S. 809 (1975).
70. 425 U.S. 748 (1976).
71. *Id.* at 759–65.
72. *Id.* at 771 n. 24, 772.
73. 433 U.S. 350 (1977).

74. *In re* R.M.J., 455 U.S. 191 (1982).
75. Zauderer v. Office of Disciplinary Counsel, 471 U.S. 626 (1985).
76. Shapero v. Kentucky Bar Ass'n., 486 U.S. 466, 473–78 (1988).
77. *Id.* at 487.
78. *Id.* at 480.
79. Peel v. Attorney Registration and Disciplinary Comm. of Ill., 496 U.S. 91 (1990).
80. *Id.* at 105.
81. *Id.* at 119.
82. *Id.* at 125.
83. 492 U.S. 469 (1989).
84. *See, e.g.*, Central Hudson Gas & Electric Corp. v. Public Service Comm'n. of New York, 447 U.S. 557 (1980).
85. 492 U.S. at 476–77.
86. *Id.* at 486–89.
87. NAACP v. Alabama ex rel. Patterson, 357 U.S. 449 (1958).
88. Bates v. Little Rock, 361 U.S. 516 (1960).
89. A more recent example of the Court's treatment of the associational rights of unions and their members, linked to closed shop claims and state "right to work" laws, may be found in Lincoln Federal Labor Union v. Northwestern Iron & Metal Co., 335 U.S. 525 (1949).
90. 485 U.S. 360 (1988).
91. *Id.* at 368.
92. *Id.* at 371–72.
93. *Id.* at 374.
94. 468 U.S. 609 (1984). For a brief review of this venture in counterpoising values, see Stanley H. Friedelbaum, *Justice William J. Brennan, Jr.: Policy-Making in the Judicial Thicket, in* THE BURGER COURT: POLITICAL AND JUDICIAL PROFILES (Charles M. Lamb and Stephen C. Halpern, eds., 1991). 109–10.
95. 481 U.S. 537 (1987).
96. *Id.* at 546.
97. *Id.* at 549.
98. 490 U.S. 19 (1989).
99. *Id.* at 28–29.

---4---

Perceptions of the Mass Media, Obscenity Questions, and Other Aspects of Press Freedom

The realization of an idealized image of a free press in a free society has always ranked high on a roster of national purposes, reflecting a romantic attachment to a hyperbolic vision of America's liberal heritage. John Peter Zenger's case, long symbolic of the right of the press to serve as an instrument of political protest, set the stage for the Revolutionary era with its emphasis on free expression and publication. Sir William Blackstone's famous treatise extolled liberty of the press as "essential to the nature of a free state." But his view of a free press lay principally in the absence of prior restraint, not in the extension of protection to those who published what was "improper, mischievous, or illegal." Press freedom did not serve to shield transgressors from suffering the consequences of their own temerity. In this light, the Sedition Act of 1798 perpetuated notions of seditious libel, restricting permissible criticism of government or its actions.

It was this legacy that cast an ominous shadow over a free press, particularly in times of turmoil. Fears of suppression recurred during and following World War I and, in a somewhat different guise, in the midst of the anti-Communist crusade associated with the McCarthy years. Throughout all of the efforts to bridle free expression, the First Amendment's guarantees were threatened, in part, by persistent linkages to the common law of defamation. The uneasy interactive relationship between expression and libel was marked by conflicting values and directions. Opposing principles and discordant applications constantly lurked just beneath the surface, albeit not at the same levels of intensity, during stressful periods in the nation's history.

LIBEL AND FIRST AMENDMENT STRICTURES

Any expectation of achieving an expansive reading of First Amendment safeguards essentially created a need to modify traditional standards of libel. The law of defamation, as it had been customarily perceived and applied, was excessively inhibiting in its effects on the output of the mass media. An early case, *Near v. Minnesota*,[1] dealt with a state law that provided for injunctive relief against "malicious, scandalous and defamatory" publications. A bare majority, speaking through Chief Justice Hughes, set aside the statute for having imposed an "unconstitutional restraint upon publication" tantamount to censorship. Yet, as late as 1952, the Court sanctioned state action against group libel which, Justice Frankfurter noted for the majority, did not warrant negative intervention deriving from the First Amendment or the liberty provision of the Fourteenth Amendment's Due Process Clause.[2] The standard adopted closely paralleled the "reasonable man test" formerly associated with Justice Holmes.

The "constitutionalization" of the law of libel came to pass in *New York Times Co. v. Sullivan*,[3] where the Court, speaking through Justice Brennan, held that the Constitution "delimits a state's power to award damages for libel in actions brought by public officials against critics of their official conduct." A rule requiring proof of actual malice was made applicable.[4] Justice Brennan went on to make reference to the alien and sedition acts with a terse notation that the unconstitutionality of the sedition law of 1798 had been amply demonstrated in the "court of history."[5] Libel, he made bold to state, had no "talismanic immunity" from constitutional limitations; even false statements were protected unless proof existed of knowing falsehood or reckless disregard of questions of verity.[6] Despite the strength of these assertions in behalf of a potent First Amendment, Justice Black took the proof of malice test to offer little more than an "evanescent protection." It was not equivalent, he averred, to an outright prohibition upon the exercise of state power in enforcing the law of civil libel in the face of the "sturdy safeguard" emanating from the First Amendment.[7]

As a concomitant of the *New York Times* rule, the public official standard was expanded to encompass a "public figure" component. Justice Harlan's plurality opinion in *Curtis Publishing Co. v. Butts*[8] articulated new, less rigorous guidelines governing the recovery of damage by public figures as distinguished from public officials. Instead of a need to provide proof of actual malice, a public figure had only to demonstrate that he or she was the victim of defamatory falsehoods whose substance posed a substantial danger to reputation "on a showing of highly unreasonable conduct constituting an extreme departure from the standards of investigation and reporting ordinarily adhered to by responsible publishers."[9] To Chief Justice Warren, who concurred in the judgment, the differentiation set out by Justice Harlan and the utilization of discrete standards of proof had "no basis in law, logic, or First Amendment policy."[10] The tenor of this assessment and the variant directions pursued by other Justices in additional opinions submitted in *Curtis Publishing* gave evidence of the doubts and indecision that prevailed in this area.

Subsequent cases sought to clarify the standards to be applied to suits instituted by public figures and to enlarge upon the role of the states, thereby permitting a partial return to more traditional gauges of libel in relation to suits by private individuals. Special protection for the media declined. The Court no longer agreed to afford unusual breadth to characterizations of a public figure. In an apparent effort to strike a feasible balance, the safeguards placed about media defendants and the rights of those purportedly maligned were brought closer to a state of equality. The notion that private individuals, unwittingly thrust into unwanted and unsought prominence, could be made the subjects of palpably intrusive and hurtful inquiries was all but abandoned.[11]

At the same time, the Court did not move to broaden the definition of publishing activities embraced within the protective overlay of the *New York Times* rule. A credit-reporting agency was held liable for damages resulting from its statements without requiring proof of actual malice. In *Dun & Bradstreet, Inc. v Greenmoss Builders*,[12] a plurality set aside any media-nonmedia dichotomy as a basis of judgment while two concurring Justices went so far as to question the fundamental principle of constitutionalizing the law of defamation.[13] Justice Powell, writing the plurality opinion, introduced still another dimension distinguishing between expressive matters of public concern and those of no more than private interest, as here, that merited assignment of reduced constitutional values. The latter, it developed, fell outside the perimeter of heightened First Amendment scrutiny that called for application of the *New York Times* standard. Instead, more conventional attention to actual injury emerged as the prevailing measure in state courts.[14] All the same, the Court refused to sanction any differentiation, for First Amendment purposes, of statements of opinion and of fact.[15]

Persistent attempts to sustain some type of protective equipoise between the press and private individuals have not resulted in a reversal of course perceptibly detrimental to the media. In *Hustler Magazine v. Falwell*,[16] a unanimous Court, speaking through Chief Justice Rehnquist, denied recovery of damages to an acknowledged public figure who charged a publisher with the intentional infliction of emotional distress. The complaint centered about an ad parody that conveyed a sexual double entendre and portrayed the persons identified in what they took to be a derogatory and decidedly offensive manner. Chief Justice Rehnquist declined to give judicial credence to this "novel" variant of defamation. To the contrary, he made reference to the *New York Times* rule, the need for the "sort of robust political debate encouraged by the First Amendment," the "truth-seeking function of the marketplace of ideas," and other aphorisms associated with expressive freedom.[17] He went on to note that a political cartoon or caricature was often neither reasoned nor evenhanded and that it might even be "outrageous" in its tone and impact. Yet the Court refused to strike down such a display regardless of its possibly adverse effects on the audience. Notwithstanding the nature of the speech, public figures must prove that the publication contains a false statement of fact, made with "actual malice" and with reckless disregard of whether it was or was not true.[18] Such close adherence to the *New York Times* standard, Chief Justice Rehnquist insisted, was needed to provide adequate "breathing space" for First Amendment freedoms.[19]

Almost two decades have passed since the *New York Times* standard was first announced. During this period, serious doubts have been raised concerning its continuing vitality as a constitutional modus operandi, yet the rule has managed to survive a number of assaults upon its viability as a determinant of First Amendment adjudicatory results. In the initial phases, much attention focused about the nature of the complainant, whether a public or a private figure. More recently, additional elements have been added to the decisional equation, namely, the nature of the speech and its status as of public or private concern. Clearly, expressive freedoms are most likely to prevail when the figure and the speech are found to be of public import. The reverse sequence, with both factors in the private mode, just as surely promises a marked diminution of First Amendment safeguards, if any are applicable, and the restoration of traditional state-espoused common-law principles of defamation.

Somewhat akin to its treatment of defamatory conduct, the Court, in *Cohen v. Cowles Media Company*,[20] considered a cause of action instituted by an informant charging newspapers with a breach of assured confidentiality. The complainant, associated with a political campaign, had disclosed derogatory materials concerning an opposition party's candidate on condition that his identity remain anonymous. Once the pledge of confidentiality had been broken, the informant was dismissed from his post. He sought damages for the loss of his position and for the reduced earning capacity that resulted. The newspapers claimed First Amendment protection from suit by reason of a presumably adverse effect upon their ability to report the news should such damages be awarded and sustained.

A defamation suit was not feasible under these circumstances because the information revealed, that is, the informant's name, was not open to challenge as untrue. Instead, the aggrieved plaintiff sought recovery under a state-law doctrine creating legal obligations to enforce the promise of confidentiality. The Supreme Court, speaking through Justice White, sustained the cause of action undertaken. No invasion of First Amendment rights was said to have occurred since the law in question was of general applicability. Any effects upon news organizations and guaranteed press freedoms were found to be no more than "incidental"; enforcement of such general laws was not subject to strict scrutiny. Justice White concluded that the law had not targeted or singled out the press, that the First Amendment does not afford the press "limitless" protection, and that it does not confer upon the news media a constitutional right to disregard promises otherwise enforceable under state law.[21]

That the common law of defamation and its linkages to the First Amendment were not far removed from the breach of promise action in *Cohen* was repeatedly alluded to and addressed, especially in the dissenting opinions. Justice Blackmun, joined by Justices Marshall and Souter, took the Court to task for permitting the state law to be used to enforce punishment of the expression of truthful information or opinion. Thus, in the absence of compelling state interests, the dissenters held, the state's action had impermissibly restricted federally secured freedom of the press.[22]

Justice Souter, joined in dissent by Justices Marshall, Blackmun, and O'Connor, declined to accept the fact of the law's general applicability to be dispositive. He went on to note that the newspapers' revelation of the informant's identity expanded the "universe of information" available to voters. Additionally, Justice Souter asserted, the injured party was not a private individual whose identity was wholly lacking in public concern. On balance, then, the state's interest in enforcing the media's promise of confidentiality was held to be "insufficient to outweigh the interest in unfettered publication of the information revealed in this case. . . ."[23]

Interestingly, the Court has moved to return defamation law (and its peripherally associated incidents) to the states without abrogating the protection provided by the First Amendment under specific conditions. The media are no longer treated as if they were inexplicably immunized from virtually all liability simply by virtue of their existence in a free society and overstated assumptions concerning their contributions and vulnerability. The byword of note has become one of accountability in the event that untoward activities violate the rights of those who may become the media's defenseless victims. If state responsibility and control have returned to consideration of the appropriate scope of freedom of the press, the attitudinal changes evidenced are not intended to be so invasive as to compromise the legitimate activities of the mass media. The public-private figure dichotomy remains, but the preservation of individual privacy rights now looms larger in the balancing test that federal courts are required to apply.

OBSCENITY AND THE FIRST AMENDMENT

Like libelous material, obscene publications traditionally have been excluded from the reach of the First Amendment's protection. Much of the influence of Victorian standards during the late nineteenth century and the first decade of the twentieth century derived, in legal terms, from the English case, *Regina v. Hicklin*,[24] that judged obscenity on the basis of its supposed effect on those in society most susceptible to base suggestion. In the United States, such a narrow view served the evangelical purposes of "Comstockery," an extremist movement named after Anthony Comstock, a self-proclaimed moral crusader. It was Comstock and his followers who brought persistent pressure to bear on federal and state legislators to secure passage of laws against the dissemination of obscene matter. These acts, with modifications, prompted a series of challenges that, by the middle years of the twentieth century, brought the quest for workable obscenity standards to the attention of the Supreme Court and, in its vanguard, began a long-term process of relaxing the rigidity of the then prevailing censorship. The modern era of definitional differentiation and interpretive labeling was about to open.

An initial effort to enumerate standards of judgment occurred in 1957[25] when the Supreme Court, speaking through Justice Brennan, explicitly reaffirmed that obscenity was not protected speech within the meaning of the First Amendment. Yet Justice Brennan noted that sex and obscenity were not synonymous, that obscene material was that which dealt with sex "in a manner appealing to prurient interest," and that all ideas "having even the slightest redeeming social importance" had the full protection of expressive guarantees. He opted for substituted guidelines to replace the *Hicklin* test—guidelines that judged obscenity by applying, for the average person, contemporary community standards to determine whether the dominant theme of materials appealed to prurient interest. If the effectiveness of these guidelines remained problematic and difficult of utilization in ensuing cases, there was no occasion to envision a return to the extremist benchmarks of Comstockery. Nonetheless, the subsequent inclusion of a so-called "pandering corollary"[26] added little of substance or procedural propriety but attached a decidedly negative hue to the ongoing judicial debate over obscenity.

A succession of cases added ponderous new twists and turns to the tortuous course of obscenity adjudications. The Burger Court, in an attempt to resolve recurring aspects of what had proved to be a complex and confounding colloquy, sought to establish "concrete guidelines" designed to isolate "hard-core" pornography from expression that merited First Amendment protection. Combining a significant modification and downgrading of the *Roth* standards as these had developed and expanded, the Court essentially sought to defer to local rather than national community standards in applying a "prurient interest" test.[27] Dissenting in one of the cases,[28] Justice Brennan concluded, somewhat belatedly it appears, that his previous efforts to fashion usable obscenity standards had failed, that they had contributed to disharmony, and that case-by-case formulations ought to be abandoned.[29] Instead, he proposed that, in the absence of distribution to juveniles or "obtrusive exposure" to nonconsenting adults, government at all levels should not be permitted to suppress sexually oriented material. Such an alternative, Justice Brennan averred, would lessen pressure on judicial resources while preserving expressive liberty and protecting essential governmental concerns.[30]

Notwithstanding Justice Brennan's dramatically simplistic proposals, the deferential guidelines adopted in the early years of the Burger Court era have remained essentially unchanged. The emphasis has shifted to a "secondary effects" analysis and to a notably less compelling protection of "lower value" communication as it relates specifically to dealers in sexually oriented material. In *City of Renton v. Playtime Theatres, Inc.*,[31] the Court considered the validity of a municipal ordinance, in effect establishing a "redlight" district by way of zoning designed to "contain" adult theaters. Justice Rehnquist, for the Court, found the city's efforts "unrelated to the suppression of free expression." Instead, the intent, by the terms of the ordinance, lay elsewhere—to prevent crime, to preserve land and neighborhood values, and, more generally, to enhance the quality of life in an urban setting. Since the promotion of these interests was "substantial," Justice Rehnquist inveighed, there was no cause to take account of the limited areas available to the purveyors of sexually explicit wares. Prohibitively high prices in the prevailing real estate market, where these existed, may have created difficulties of procurement, but these did "not give rise to a First Amendment violation."[32] To the contrary, Justice Brennan, joined in dissent by Justice Marshall, was critical of the Court's resort to a secondary effects standard. The city's regulatory venture, he noted, was founded principally in the content of the films displayed, contrary to First Amendment guarantees; thus it revealed hostility to the views expressed.

If theaters and places of public entertainment may be subjected to restrictive zoning provisions, is a more expansive resort to the state's police power presumptively valid in relation to bookstores? The question arose in *Arcara v. Cloud Books, Inc.*[33] when an establishment was closed as a public health nuisance. An "adult" bookstore, the Court declared in sustaining the closure, constituted only a segment of the physical premises otherwise devoted to prostitution and other hazardous pursuits. Since any expressive elements involved were not significant, Chief Justice Burger maintained, the First Amendment was "not implicated by the enforcement of a public health regulation of general application" where "respondents happen to sell books."[34] Justice Blackmun, joined by

Justices Brennan and Marshall, dissented, taking issue with the Court's approval of the state's suppression of speech by invoking public health concerns. When the state impairs activities protected by the First Amendment, Justice Blackmun protested, the state must demonstrate, "at a minimum, that it has chosen the least restrictive means of pursuing its legitimate objectives."[35] Justice O'Connor, joined by Justice Stevens, concurred in the Court's judgment but cautioned that any "pretextual use" of a comparable nuisance provision would implicate First Amendment interests.[36]

While some members of the Court continue to have reservations concerning the use of otherwise permissible police power principles to "rein in" arguably pornographic enterprises, the *Miller* tests, though minimally addressed, do not err as heavily on community involvement as the zoning and public health cases would seem to suggest. Justice White, writing for the Court in *Pope v. Illinois*,[37] distinguished the three prongs set out in *Miller* with a terse notation that the first two—determining an appeal to prurient interest and patent offensiveness—were issues for juries to decide applying contemporary community standards. But the third prong, weighing literary, artistic, political, or scientific values, fell into the category of ideas, beyond majoritarian approval as such, but within First Amendment parameters, subject to inquiry measured against a "reasonable person" criterion.[38] Justice Scalia, concurring, expressed serious doubt that values could be objectively evaluated by way of litigational techniques.[39] Justice Stevens, among the dissenters in *Pope*, sought to preclude criminal regulation of obscenity under the First Amendment, citing the futility of a "reasonable person" standard.[40]

A state's effort to include obscenity violations within the offenses noted in a Racketeer Influenced and Corrupt Organizations (RICO) statute was sustained in *Fort Wayne Books, Inc. v. Indiana*.[41] Justice White, for the Court, held that a criminal act, applicable to booksellers, admittedly might promote self-censorship and inhibit the dissemination of nonobscene materials. Yet, he asserted, the possibility of such results did not suffice to render the law unconstitutional under existing precedents. Justice Stevens, joined in dissent by Justices Brennan and Marshall, took exception to any scheme that might have an adverse impact on the distribution of constitutionally protected publications.

In *Sable Communications of California, Inc. v. FCC*,[42] the Court distinguished the regulation of "indecent" from obscene material. First Amendment protection extended, Justice White asserted for the Court, to the former as expression. Consequently, the indecency section of the communications act, as amended by Congress, was found to be unconstitutional in relation to the transmission of telephone messages. Adult conversations could not be restricted, White averred, to what is suitable for children. Justice Brennan, joined by Justices Marshall and Stevens, agreed with the majority's conclusions concerning indecent matter, but he dissented with respect to what appeared to be a permissible ban on obscene communications.

The question of censorship in relation to live performances arose in *Barnes v. Glen Theatre, Inc.*,[43] a controversial and inconclusive decision related to nude dancing, public indecency, and the First Amendment. Chief Justice Rehnquist, announcing the judgment of the Court and submitting no more than a plurality opinion, conceded that the performances at issue constituted expressive conduct but, as he put it, behavior "within the outer perimeters of the First Amendment, though we view it as only marginally so."[44] Applying a four-part test derived from a Vietnam era draft-card burning case,[45] the plurality found the state law justified despite the incidental limitations on expressive activity that it conveyed. The weight of the police power came into play, Chief Justice Rehnquist asserted, in the protection of order and morality. The evil sought to be dealt with was public nudity, not erotic dancing. And, the plurality concluded, it was "without cavil" that the statute had been "narrowly tailored."

The several individual opinions set out in *Barnes* offer a discerning cross-section of the Court's fragmented approaches to proscribed sexual displays. Justice Scalia, concurring, criticized what he took to be the plurality's endorsement of an intermediate level of First Amendment scrutiny in the circumstances. To Scalia, the state was regulating conduct, not expression, and so the First Amendment was not implicated.[46] Justice Souter, in a concurring opinion, was less certain of the absence of First Amendment guarantees when nudity was combined with expressive activity. There was, he noted, a "degree" of constitutional protection involved in a performance advancing eroticism as expressive content. What warranted state intervention, however, was a valid effort to combat pernicious secondary effects, such as prostitution and associated crimes, linked to establishments that fostered the conduct under review.[47] It is clear that First Amendment overtones lay at the periphery of these exercises in decision making. What remains in doubt is the applicability of such soundings and the measure of protection that they extended.

To Justice White, joined in dissent by Justices Marshall, Blackmun, and Stevens, nonobscene nude dancing exhibited "distinct communicative aspects" that conveyed a message within the ambit of First Amendment protection. Such a performance, therefore, could not be "pigeonholed" as conduct apart from its expressive component. Justice White admitted that the dance routines might not be "high art, to say the least, and may not appeal to the Court. . . . " But, he inveighed, this was not a basis for the distortion and abandonment of "settled doctrine." As Justice White perceived it, the performances involved targeted expressive activity and, indeed, it was designated as a crime because of the message that it conveyed.[48]

Despite intermittent and, at times, fervent efforts by the Justices, definitions of obscenity and, more recently, of indecency, remain as elusive as they were when the Court first undertook its modern ventures in the late 1950s. Refinements have been introduced along the way; new categorizations have been utilized; and less intrusive resorts to the state's police power have been brought into play. Outright interdiction of expression is frowned upon as more subtle devices take on more sophisticated forms. Yet fundamental impediments remain amidst settings promotive of questions that defy easy solutions. If, as repeated forays continue, obscenity remains theoretically beyond First Amendment safeguards, poorly disguised replicas seem to qualify for a limited degree of constitutional protection. Like its predecessors, the Rehnquist Court displays a reluctance to disavow unremittingly the sanctity of expression no matter how disfavored the source may be.

UNCONVENTIONAL ASPECTS OF PRESS FREEDOM

If the obscenity-indecency cases persist in being mired in uncertainty and circumvention of the actual issues presented, an additional element is cast into the decisional equation when First Amendment protection of media interests is weighed against the formidable bulwark of fair trial guarantees embodied in the Sixth Amendment. The free press/fair trial dichotomy reflects an impressive history of recurring conflict, but one marked by disarray in the formulation of convincing, long-term guidelines. Where the two constitutional provisions appear to collide, it seems, there can be no easy resolution short of the sacrifice of the one or the other. Judges, advocates, and bar associations have long sought to assure the sanctity of the trial process. At the same time, news media representatives have repeatedly asserted the social utility of the reporting functions of a free press. Is an accommodation possible, no matter how imperfect, without inducing an adverse impact affecting either?

The status of out-of-court comment in relation to judicial proceedings has often been debated, especially as it touches upon the reach of the contempt power. Congress became involved during the early years of the nineteenth century when an open confrontation developed between an attorney named Luke Lawless and a federal judge, James H. Peck of Missouri. The outcome provided little guidance that survived the controversy, much less the century.[49]

Closer to contemporary events was the application of a "clear and present danger" test as a measure in appeals from contempt convictions linked to criticism of judicial activities.[50] While the Court initially moved to discourage a resort to the contempt power as a means of preventing out-of-court comment,[51] a succeeding series of cases witnessed at least a partial turnabout to combat what was termed "trial by newspaper"—a process that threatened to undermine the independence and integrity of the judiciary in providing for a fair trial free of extraneous influences and pressures.[52] In the much-noted, highly volatile case of *Sheppard v. Maxwell*,[53] the Court attempted to meet due process requirements by proscribing extra-judicial statements from trial participants. Press correspondents were warned of improprieties, but the imposition of legal sanctions was avoided despite activities that concededly might have prejudiced a fair trial.

Divisions in the Rehnquist Court have been great, resulting in inconclusive outcomes, when out-of-court comment issues have arisen. In *Gentile v. State Bar of Nevada*,[54] an attorney was reprimanded for having held a press conference following his client's indictment on criminal charges. A claim that his free speech rights had been violated was rejected by the state supreme court. In reversing these findings, a bifurcated Court determined that the rule that had served as the basis of the action against the lawyer was void for vagueness. Justice Kennedy held that its "safe harbor" provision had failed to provide fair notice and that its imprecision might have led to discriminatory enforcement. There was danger, Kennedy noted, that the rule had created "a trap for the wary as well as the unwary."[55]

A different majority, with Chief Justice Rehnquist as its spokesperson, concluded that the "substantial likelihood of material prejudice" test, applied in this case, conformed to First Amendment tenets. The need to assure a fair trial remained a legitimate basis for state regulation. Yet the limitations on speech were appropriately "narrow and necessary." The standard applied, Chief Justice Rehnquist asserted, struck a "constitutionally permissible balance between the First Amendment rights of attorneys in pending cases and the state's interest in fair trials." The regulation of speech could be achieved under a "less demanding" test than that established for the press.[56] Justice O'Connor's votes were crucial to the positions of both factions.[57]

Returning to a number of themes previously explored in *Sheppard v. Maxwell*, the Court in *Mu'Min v. Virginia*[58] considered the effects of adverse pretrial publicity on jury selection in a capital murder case. At issue, perhaps more explicitly than in earlier cases, was the impact of such exposure upon a defendant's Sixth Amendment guarantee to trial by an impartial jury. Chief Justice Rehnquist, writing for the Court, denied that either the Sixth Amendment or the Fourteenth Amendment Due Process Clause required a trial judge to question prospective jurors concerning the specific contents of news reports which they may have read or heard. Such an inquiry, he stressed, was not a constitutional requirement.[59] To Justice Marshall, joined by Justices Blackmun and Stevens in dissent, the majority's reasoning had turned a critical constitutional mandate into a "hollow formality."[60] The measure of deference accorded the trial judge was especially unacceptable, Marshall protested, since a requirement of individual "content" questioning was indispensable in this case that, as Marshall viewed it, was "essentially one of first impression."[61]

If the press, like jury members, face notable impediments or exacting scrutiny in the interest of a fair trial, the reach of the First Amendment's protection of expression and publication is also limited in special situations such as a school environment. In *Bethel School District No. 403 v. Fraser*,[62] a student, in the course of a speech nominating a fellow student for a school's election office, made untoward sexual remarks that led to disciplinary proceedings against him. His reliance on First Amendment rights was sustained in a federal district court and in an appeals court review. But reversal followed in the Supreme Court. A seven-to-two decision reproached the trial judge for having failed to distinguish political expression from sexual content. Chief Justice Burger sustained the school district's resort to sanctions for "offensively lewd and indecent speech" unrelated, as the majority construed it, to any "political viewpoint."[63] Justice Marshall, dissenting, took issue with the penalty imposed since disruption of the school's educational activities had not been demonstrated.[64] Justice Stevens' dissent noted that the student did not have reason to expect the punitive consequences that followed his delivery of the speech in question.[65]

More disturbing than *Fraser*, and overtly directed to the abridgment of press freedom, was the Court's subsequent action in *Hazelwood School District v. Kuhlmeier*[66] where Justice White, for the majority, sustained the educators' editorial control of the contents of a school newspaper. Officials had ordered deletion of accounts of teenage pregnancy and the effects of divorce on children. Such control did not violate the First Amendment, Justice White argued, when the expressive activities are school-sponsored and "reasonably related to legitimate pedagogical concerns."[67] Justice Brennan, dissenting, objected to the Court's indulgence in the suppression of student expression on grounds of "mere incompatibility with the school's pedagogical message."[68] The intervention condoned by the Court, it appeared from an aggregate of the opinions, was far more pervasive than that countenanced in *Fraser* where it was the manner of presentation, not the content, that was found to be offensive.

Justice White's attempt in *Hazelwood* to differentiate permissible personal from school-sponsored speech[69] offered no more than a distinction without a difference. It was impractical to assert that individual student expression could be equated with an article published in a school newspaper. The willingness of administrators not to censor the ideas being disseminated by an individual had little impact upon the overall currents of expression. It was the school newspaper or a comparable forum that provided a central outlet for advocacy, commentary, or critical assessments of social issues. Educators in *Hazelwood* served as censors, acting in behalf of the state, not as private publishers. Thus, the First Amendment came into play even if the rights guaranteed were held to be of a lower ranking than the rights of adults in less confining settings.

One of the few positive by-products of the Court's several opinions in *Hazelwood* was its reaffirmation of the findings in *Tinker v. Des Moines School District*.[70] The famous anti-Vietnam conflict armband decision sustained expression, even within the special bounds of the school environment, so long as expression (akin to pure speech in this instance) was "divorced from actually or potentially disruptive conduct."[71] Judicial credence was afforded the aphorism that students do not abandon their constitutional rights at the "schoolhouse gate." If *Tinker* remained minimally vibrant as a controlling precedent, no adequate predicate existed for assuring expressive activities that failed to be in accord with a school's "educational mission."

An overall evaluation of the Rehnquist Court's performance in regard to press freedom reveals mixed patterns. Discernible trends loom, but none has been carried to a point that suggests definitive guidelines with strong elements of predictability. Instead, tentative judgments recur in an area marked by sensitivity and historic vestiges that cannot be overlooked despite what appear to be the proclivities of a conservative majority. While Justice Black's long-time dalliance with an "absolutist" approach to First Amendment expressive liberty has never been taken seriously, the current Court's apparent willingness to embrace constitutional relativism also strikes a note of disbelief and even of charlatanism among Justices said to be dedicated philosophically to a return to "original intent." The breadth of press freedom remains as incalculable and often as puzzling as it has been in the past.

What are the emergent trends that have come to the fore and that seem to have reasonable prospects of enduring? The *New York Times* rule in relation to the common law of defamation and the First Amendment has survived many incursions and, though less vigorous than in its early stages, its recent applications strike a workable balance between the preservation of expressive freedom and the privacy rights of individuals. By contrast, efforts to define obscenity have declined in number and in vigor, if they have not been wholly spurned. In their place, the Court has turned to examine alternative methods, such as zoning, intended to resolve problems of "indecency" by way of commonplace resorts to the states' police power. When the First and Sixth Amendments are posited as competing requisites with respect to the free press/fair trial quandary, the results have been less conclusive. If anything, fair trial seems to be preponderant in the decisional equation. And the extent of freedom in such an unconventional context as the restrictive environment of the public schools is truncated at best. Thus, an uncertain moderation prevails throughout all phases of expressive liberty though, unlike changeable tendencies evident elsewhere, tenets of press freedom remain secure and beyond reproof in a constitutional sense.

NOTES

1. 283 U.S. 697 (1931).
2. Beauharnais v. Illinois, 343 U.S. 250 (1952).
3. 376 U.S. 254 (1964).
4. *Id.* at 279, 283.
5. *Id.* at 276.
6. *Id.* at 269, 279–80.
7. *Id.* at 293–97.
8. 388 U.S. 130 (1967).
9. *Id.* at 155.
10. *Id.* at 163.
11. *See, e.g.*, Time, Inc. v. Firestone, 424 U.S. 448 (1976); Wolston v. Reader's Digest Ass'n., 443 U.S. 157 (1979). *Cf.* the Court's extension of procedural protection to publishers in Philadelphia Newspapers, Inc. v. Hepps, 475 U.S. 767 (1986).
12. 472 U.S. 749 (1985).
13. Chief Justice Burger and Justice White concurred in separate opinions.
14. 472 U.S. 758–761.
15. Milkovich v. Lorain Journal Co., 497 U.S. 1 (1990).
16. 485 U.S. 46 (1988).
17. *Id.* at 50–52.
18. *Id.* at 53–56.
19. *Id.* at 52. Additional references to the *New York Times* guidelines occurred in Masson v. New Yorker Magazine, Inc., 115 L. Ed. 2d 447 (1991). Here the Court dealt with charges that quoted material had been deliberately altered. Conformably to the *New York Times* rule, the Court noted, "a deliberate alteration of the words uttered . . . does not equate with knowledge of falsity . . . unless the alteration results in a material change in the meaning conveyed by the statement." *Id.* at 473.
20. 115 L. Ed. 2d 586 (1991).
21. *Id.* at 596–98.
22. *Id.* at 599–601.
23. *Id.* at 602–3.
24. L.R. 3 Q.B. 360 (1868).
25. Roth v. United States, 354 U.S. 476 (1957).
26. Ginsburg v. United States, 383 U.S. 463 (1966). *See also* two companion cases, A Book Named "John Cleland's Memoirs of a Woman of Pleasure" v. Attorney General, 383 U.S. 413 (1966) and Mishkin v. New York, 383 U.S. 502 (1966).
27. Miller v. California, 413 U.S. 15 (1973).
28. Paris Adult Theatre I v. Slaton, 413 U.S. 49 (1973).
29. *Id.* at 73.
30. *Id.* at 113–14.
31. 475 U.S. 41 (1986).

32. *Id.* at 50–54.
33. 478 U.S. 697 (1986).
34. *Id.* at 707.
35. *Id.* at 710.
36. *Id.* at 708.
37. 481 U.S. 497 (1987).
38. *Id.* at 501.
39. *Id.* at 505.
40. *Id.* at 511–13.
41. 489 U.S. 46 (1989).
42. 492 U.S. 115 (1989).
43. 115 L. Ed. 2d 504 (1991).
44. *Id.* at 511.
45. United States v. O'Brien, 391 U.S. 367 (1968).
46. 115 L. Ed. 2d at 520–21.
47. *Id.* at 522–23.
48. *Id.* at 528–31.
49. Judge Peck was impeached, but subsequently acquitted in early 1831 by a close vote. See STANLEY H. FRIEDELBAUM, CONTEMPORARY CONSTITUTIONAL LAW: CASE STUDIES IN THE JUDICIAL PROCESS (1972), 641–42.
50. Bridges v. California, 314 U.S. 252 (1941).
51. *See, e.g.*, Craig v. Harney, 331 U.S. 367 (1947).
52. Irvin v. Dowd, 366 U.S. 717 (1961); Rideau v. Louisiana, 373 U.S. 723 (1963); Estes v. Texas, 381 U.S. 532 (1965).
53. 384 U.S. 333 (1966).
54. 115 L. Ed. 2d 888 (1991).
55. *Id.* at 906–908.
56. *Id.* at 923–24. *See* Nebraska Press Ass'n. v. Stuart, 427 U.S. 539 (1976).
57. 115 L. Ed. 2d at 927–28.
58. 114 L. Ed. 2d 493 (1991).
59. *Id.* at 505–9.
60. *Id.* at 511.
61. *Id.* at 515–16.
62. 478 U.S. 675 (1986).
63. *Id.* at 685.
64. *Id.* at 690.
65. *Id.* at 691–93.
66. 484 U.S. 260 (1988).
67. *Id.* at 273.
68. *Id.* at 279–80.
69. *Id.* at 270–72.
70. 393 U.S. 503 (1969).
71. *Id.* at 505.

5

The Religion Clauses: Perennial Themes, Unsettled Directions

The Framers' dedication to a rigorous separation of church and state was evident in the original text of the Constitution. In terms reflective of a pioneering spirit and of exceptional liberality of opinion even for the Age of Enlightenment, Article VI provided that "no religious test shall ever be required as a qualification to any office or public trust under the United States." The test oath ban thus prescribed was readily adopted by the delegates and, since its introduction more than two centuries ago, scant references to it have appeared in the annals of the Supreme Court.

When, following the ratification of the Constitution and the initial implementation of its provisions, the First Congress turned to the drafting of the Bill of Rights, a greater degree of discord became evident. That some disagreement marked what were to be the Religion Clauses of the First Amendment appeared from the debates in both houses. Perhaps the salient reason for approval of the vigorous language of the Establishment and Free Exercise Clauses lay in the acknowledged inapplicability of these provisions, like the Bill of Rights generally, to the states. Established churches, rooted in the colonial experience, were to be found in a number of states. Consequently, members of Congress, especially in the Senate, were willing to support strong prohibitions only on the assumption that the provisions would be applicable solely to the national government, not to the states. Few feared that Congress would act to establish a national church. Guarantees of free exercise of religion were also taken to be beyond federal encroachment. Initially, therefore, the Religion Clauses were looked upon as significant deterrents binding upon the nation, not as operative clauses that would substantially affect practices in the states.

With the exception of a scattering of cases decided during the late nineteenth century and the early decades of the twentieth century,[1] the Religion Clauses did not give rise to a volume of litigation comparable to that which characterized other areas of American jurisprudence. Popular misgivings over the spread of polygamy among Mormons in Utah proved to be ephemeral. The Court's response, though negative, had little long-term impact on contemporary doctrinal formulations. Apart from such efforts to outlaw "deviant" social customs and conventions, case law offered little that was lasting. The Court referred to a "religious nation" theme on three occasions, most recently by Justice Douglas in 1952 when he announced that "we are a religious people whose institutions presuppose a Supreme Being."[2] Such avowals and dicta of religiosity have not been repeated, although a number of cases arising under the Establishment Clause have come to affirm, more often implicitly, similar asseverations.

A continuum of developmental patterns affecting religion did not come to pass until the 1940s. The modern era of the Religion Clauses required an express judicial acknowledgment of their applicability to state proceedings. In *Cantwell v. Connecticut*,[3] and *Everson v. Board of Education*,[4] the Court avouched the "absorption" of these clauses by way of the concept of liberty embodied in the Fourteenth Amendment. Thenceforth, reference to these segments of the First Amendment proceeded in a variety of circumstances hitherto left without redress except in the state courts and premised on counterpart provisions of the state constitutions. *Cantwell* opened a period of judicial ferment and experimentation centering about the Jehovah's Witnesses cases. Free exercise of religion was overextended to avoid any negative implications concerning the status of a much-decried minority. Yet the distinctions sanctioned, overtly favoring religious expression, raised serious questions touching upon the separation principle since government, in effect, had moved to provide special encouragement to adherents of a particular religious sect.[5]

Whether or not those who crafted the Religion Clauses were aware of the enigma that they had created, the First Amendment, despite its semantic breadth, conveyed an inner tension that could not be concealed nor readily eschewed. The potential conflicts did not become manifest until the clauses were given practical effect in state proceedings. On successive occasions, beginning in the middle decades of the twentieth century, the state's police power had to be weighed against broad standards of religious expression and separation. It proved to be unmistakable that elements of incompatibility loomed in case after case; that an accommodation of opposing precepts had to be undertaken; and that the outcome, more often than not, would serve to contract perceptibly the reach of either free exercise or establishment. A perfect fit, while perhaps theoretically possible, was not likely in resolving the demanding and vexing controversies that increasingly came before the Supreme Court.

From the early years in *Everson*, no less a stalwart than Justice Black embraced two positions that were fundamentally incompatible. The wall-of-separation metaphor, a much-quoted invention of Thomas Jefferson dating from a letter of 1802, was cited by Justice Black as a controlling limitation on state power. Yet his opinion, sustaining state reimbursement of bus transportation costs for parents whose children attended private schools, was predicated on a simulated theory of neutrality to believers and nonbelievers alike. The state could not be an adversary to handicap religion any more than it might favor it.[6] It remained problematic, as the dissenters, led by Justice Rutledge, viewed it, for the strict neutrality required by the First Amendment to serve as the basis for an arrangement that affected matters of private right.[7]

The turn away from this version of "benign" neutrality occurred the following year when the Court, in *McCollum v. Board of*

Education,[8] invalidated a released-time program of religious instruction conducted in the public schools. Justice Black, writing once again for the Court, sought to differentiate his findings in the bus case from those set out in *McCollum*. To Black, utilization of the public school system to assist religious groups to spread their faith ran contrary to the notion of a wall of separation and the basic principles propounded in *Everson*. Justice Frankfurter, concurring in *McCollum*, referred to divisive forces lurking in the educational system, coupled with what he took to be "ominous" breaches in Jefferson's wall and elements antagonistic to a "spacious conception" of separation.[9] Though perhaps overstated, Frankfurter's opinion approached an "absolutist" interpretation of the Establishment Clause.

Uncertainties inherent in the Court's changing formulations and weighting of the Religion Clauses were apparent in subsequent decisions. In *Zorach v. Clauson*,[10] a released-time case decided just four years after *McCollum*, the Court sustained the program with references to vacuous distinctions premised on religious instruction conducted off rather than on the public school premises. A more accurate explanation (and one closer to reality) lay in Justice Douglas' de facto repudiation of *McCollum*, predicated on a reworking of neutrality but with the Court serving as an agency of accommodation, not as a protagonist of an exacting, scrupulously enforced separation. Justice Jackson's description of the majority opinion in *Zorach* as "passionate dialectics" best connoted the unsettled course of the Court's progress and the indeterminate decisions that predictably lay ahead.

Challenges to the constitutionality of Sunday closing laws, long a source of controversy, brought the Religion Clauses within the vortex of a series of cases that, if anything, heightened existing tensions. Establishment issues were mitigated by a peculiar characterization of the Blue Laws as exercises of the police power not to aid religion but to "set aside a day of rest and recreation"[11]—a day marked by tranquility and opportunities for family activities and "togetherness." Free exercise objections were less easily dismissed although, in a plurality opinion, Chief Justice Warren called attention to an "indirect burden" test regarding religious observance.[12] Should alternatives be examined, the plurality noted, a one-day-in-seven law or an exemption for Sabbatarians was held to be unsatisfactory.

A notable lack of constancy marked treatment of the Religion Clauses during ensuing decades. The Bible-reading cases[13] and such anomolies as a state's ban on the teaching of evolution[14] led to reasonably consistent and minimally divisive holdings linked to the Establishment Clause. Less satisfying in their long-term sweep and applicability were decisions resulting from challenges to statutes affording aid to religiously affiliated schools, particularly funding arguably unrelated to instruction. *Lemon v. Kurtzman*,[15] not a highly controversial case in itself, led to the introduction of a formula of judgment that seemed appropriate and serviceable on the face of it, but which ultimately came to be the source of continuing discord and inconsistency.

Chief Justice Burger, writing for the Court in *Lemon*, attempted to summarize "cumulative criteria" developed by the Court over the years. Three tests emerged, providing standards against which a statute challenged under the Religion Clauses was to be measured: (1) the act was required to have a secular legislative purpose; (2) its principal or primary effect ought neither to advance nor to inhibit religion; and (3) it could not foster an excessive governmental "entanglement" with religion. If, as subsequent cases seemed to suggest, these simplistic criteria were inviting, the conclusory effects of their application to specific factual conditions proved to be no more adequate and convincing than previous tests had been. The Religion Clauses defied the effort to reduce unexpectedly complex language to straightforward, readily construed rules.

When, in *Wallace v. Jaffree*,[16] the Court invalidated a state's requirement of a moment of silence for prayer or meditation at the opening of each school day, several Justices took the occasion to express misgivings regarding *Lemon's* three-pronged test. Justice O'Connor, concurring, suggested that the standards be "reexamined and refined" to make them useful in the process of constitutional adjudication.[17] More pointedly, Justice Rehnquist objected to the *Lemon* guidelines as such. As he perceived them, they had been crafted from a "historically faulty doctrine" and had caused the Court to "fracture into unworkable plurality opinions" without yielding principled results.[18]

Recurring misgivings regarding *Lemon* came to light in separate opinions submitted in *Edwards v. Aguillard,*[19] setting aside a state's "creationism" act as violative of the Establishment Clause. Justice Scalia, joined in dissent by Chief Justice Rehnquist, was especially censorious in his assessment. In particular, he selected for critical notice the "purpose" test (the first prong of *Lemon*), which he declared, "exacerbates the tension" between the two Religion Clauses. Previously, Justice O'Connor, in the Pawtucket crèche case, *Lynch v. Donnelly,*[20] had proposed an endorsement alternative as a bridge to maintain the purpose prong of *Lemon* while modifying its effects. She suggested that an appropriate inquiry was whether government intended to convey a "message of . . . endorsement or disapproval of religion."[21] It was the endorsement corollary that moved to the forefront of the Court's consideration in weighing the future prospects of *Lemon.*

A second crèche case, *Allegheny County v. American Civil Liberties Union,*[22] led to unwonted results centering about the constitutionality of holiday displays located on public property. A crèche, placed inside a courthouse without decorations arguably secular in nature, was held to be violative of the Establishment Clause by reason of its physical setting. *Lynch,* Justice Blackmun wrote for the majority in *Allegheny County,* teaches that government may celebrate Christmas "in some manner and form, but not in a way that endorses Christian doctrine."[23] By contrast, the combined display in front of a city-county building of a menorah, a Christmas tree, and a sign saluting liberty were taken to be part of a "winter-holiday" season exhibition that met the requirement of a "secular celebration" of Christmas. Justice Blackmun made much of Justice O'Connor's reliance on an endorsement test in *Lynch,* the essentials of which he sought to apply in *Allegheny County.* The test, Justice Blackmun went on to note, provides a "sound analytical framework" for an evaluation of governmental use of religious symbols.[24]

Justice O'Connor, in a concurring opinion joined by Justices Brennan and Stevens, took the occasion to elaborate upon the endorsement standard and to amplify its scope and objectives. She reiterated the need to meet the requirements of a pluralistic society as it exemplified the religious diversity of its members. If government is to be neutral, Justice O'Connor stressed, it must do so by conveying a message of pluralism and freedom to choose. She wrote of the importance of "contextual sensitivity," focusing on specific practices in particular physical settings that determine whether an activity has had the purpose or effect of endorsing religion. The endorsement test, as she perceived it, protects, not impedes, religious liberty "so precious" to the citizenry.[25]

Although Justice Brennan appeared to have subscribed to Justice O'Connor's endorsement test, he wrote separately in *Allegheny County* (with Justices Marshall and Stevens). Justice Brennan was not persuaded that the "uncritical acceptance" of religious pluralism would be agreeable to a host of faiths often hostile to one another. He doubted that the inclusiveness proposed would be a "benign or beneficent" celebration of pluralism. Instead, he pointed out, it might well constitute interference in religious affairs precluded by the Establishment Clause.[26] Justice Stevens, joined by Justices Brennan and Marshall, expressed agreement with most of Brennan's opinion but with an admonition that the Establishment Clause should be viewed as having created a "strong presumption" against the publicly sanctioned display of all religious symbols.

Justice Kennedy, in a strident opinion joined by Chief Justice Rehnquist and Justices White and Scalia, was particularly critical of the endorsement test applied by the majority. He termed it "flawed in its fundamentals," "unworkable in practice," and "every bit as troubling as the bizarre result" that it had produced in this case. Justice Kennedy accused the Court of a "latent hostility" or "callous indifference" toward religion, contrary to a tradition of accommodation and acknowledgment.[27] Justice Blackmun, openly displeased by Kennedy's remarks, took the unusual step of responding to them in forceful language included in the majority opinion. Blackmun denounced Kennedy as having embraced a position that would "gut the core" of the Establishment Clause. In unusually blunt terms, Blackmun characterized Kennedy's accusations "as offensive as they are absurd."[28]

Has the endorsement corollary to the *Lemon* test engaged the Court in a salutary and capacious dialogue that will enhance the Establishment Clause? If the divisiveness evidenced in *Allegheny County* serves as a harbinger of future events, a resort to endorsement promises little more than previous formulas toward the achievement of a consensus and the building of positive judgmental models. With the departure of Justice Brennan in 1990, the Justices appeared to be evenly divided in regard to the standards to be applied. Justices Souter and Thomas, whose views remain largely unknown with respect to the Establishment Clause, hold a significant key to projected patterns, the doctrinal structures that may emerge, and the prospects for the separation principle as it has evolved, with intermittent alterations and divergences, since absorption first occurred in the late 1940s.

The future of endorsement remains in jeopardy; its survival, in unalloyed form, is tenuous at best. At least four members of the Court subscribe to a version of accommodation that suggests an indulgence in religious observances. Yet it is not clear that these developments presage a renaissance for the Free Exercise Clause of the First Amendment. The inverse effects of and the instances of antagonism deriving from the Religion Clauses have long been demonstrated. All the same, recent experiences with Free Exercise do not support an anticipated resuscitation of expansive displays of tolerance for diverse religious adherents. Instead, the growth of positive Free Exercise precedents has been halting and far less effusive than the dilution of Establishment Clause doctrinal advances would seem to suggest.

Almost as a collateral aside in an ever-controversial and often barbed educational context, the Court concluded in *Widmar v. Vincent*[29] that a state university could not deny student religious groups the use of university buildings when secular groups were permitted to conduct meetings in such facilities. Presumed efforts to avoid Establishment Clause violations did not serve to justify discrimination against religious speech. Provision of a neutral forum available to a "broad class of nonreligious as well as religious speakers," Justice Powell noted, did not project an "imprimatur" of state approval.[30] An "equal access" policy was said to satisfy

Lemon's three-pronged test. Attempts by the state to exceed the separation of church and state secured by the Establishment Clause, Justice Powell warned, were not compelling enough to warrant a noncontent-neutral regulation of speech.[31] Predicated on the Court's findings in *Widmar* and its emphasis on a free speech component, Congress passed an "equal access" bill in 1984, extending to public high school students the same rights of access to religiously oriented meetings as those afforded persons enrolled at colleges and universities. Schools receiving federal funds might not deny equal access provided that the meetings were not sponsored by educational authorities, attendance was voluntary, and the initial impetus came from students. Despite what would appear to have been Supreme Court endorsement of the legislation enacted, continuing unrest was evident in some schools regarding implementation of the Equal Access Act of 1984.[32] That the Court would need to confront and to resolve a variety of challenges to the statute seemed unavoidable.

In *Board of Education of Westside Community Schools v. Mergens*,[33] the Court sustained the equal access law in response to a series of objections, both statutory and constitutional. Justice O'Connor, writing for the Court in relation to questions of statutory construction, found that a religious club, like other noncurriculum-related groups, could not be excluded under the terms of the act. It was entitled to meet and to function as a "limited open forum" described in the law. The Court did not reach the question whether the denial of equal access violated the free speech or free exercise clauses of the First Amendment.

Beyond the meanings assigned the statute and its application, the Court in *Mergens* was so divided as to preclude a majority opinion. Justice O'Connor, joined by Chief Justice Rehnquist and Justices White and Blackmun, returned to the endorsement corollary as the basis for the conclusion that no violation of the Establishment Clause had occurred. Looking to previous precedents, the plurality held that private speech endorsing religion was not forbidden by the Establishment Clause; that, by contrast, it was protected by the Free Speech and Free Exercise Clauses. Student speech, permitted on a nondiscriminatory basis, did not represent the school's endorsement or support. In sum, Justice O'Connor argued, secondary school students were not likely to confuse equal access with state sponsorship of religion.[34] Justice Kennedy, joined by Justice Scalia, again refused to subscribe to the endorsement test, finding it excessively broad and unnecessarily limiting in the restrictions that it placed on the reach of government activities.[35] Contrarily, Justice Marshall, joined by Justice Brennan, called for an explicit disassociation from religious speech and the goals of the group as well as an affirmative disclaimer of any endorsement of the club if the act was to survive an Establishment Clause assault.[36]

If the equal access proviso succeeded in meeting Establishment Clause criteria, previous cases had raised the issue of the exemption of religious organizations from prohibitions against religious discrimination set out in the Civil Rights Act of 1964. A church claimed such immunity following the discharge of an employee for having failed to meet the requirement of church membership. Should the church be permitted to proceed unscathed, the employee argued, the protection provided would represent governmental intervention in behalf of religion and constitute a violation of the Establishment Clause. A unanimous Court, in *Corporation of the Presiding Bishop of Church of Jesus Christ of Latter-Day Saints v. Amos*,[37] speaking through Justice White, found no Establishment Clause infirmity, holding that there was "ample room" for an accommodation of religion.

Individual opinions reflected more emphatically the problems inherent in what otherwise appeared to be a conventional resolution of the issues. Justice Brennan, concurring and joined by Justice Marshall, expressed a preference for application of the exemption only to religious activities; but, he conceded, attempts to distinguish between secular and religious practices might have introduced serious "entanglement" concerns.[38] Justice O'Connor, concurring separately, observed that the actions condoned did, in fact, serve to advance religion. What saved the provision, in her view, was the absence of a "message of endorsement" of religion "perceived by an objective observer, acquainted with the text, legislative history, and implementation of the statute."[39] That the secular/religious dichotomy remained is evident from the caveats noted. Whether, in subsequent cases, the nebulous dividing line would be crossed and a religious organization, seeking immunity from plainly secular infractions, would be denied the exemption and made to conform continues to be problematic. Should the latter occur, significant "entanglement" questions might arise and prompt Establishment Clause complications intrinsically more compelling and formidable than those encountered.

Notions of accommodation failed to suffice the following year when, in *Texas Monthly, Inc. v. Bullock*,[40] the Court held unconstitutional a state sales tax exemption for periodicals published or distributed by a religious faith and consisting of writings promoting that faith. Since the exemption applied to purveyors of materials advancing the tenets of a religious faith and was denied to other publishers, it violated the Establishment Clause. Justice Brennan, writing for a plurality joined by Justices Marshall and Stevens, distinguished *Corporation of the Presiding Bishop* as having "prevented potentially serious encroachments on protected religious freedoms."[41] The tax exemption, by contrast, did not remove any impositions on religious activity while favoring religious adherents, providing a "blatant endorsement" of religion, and risking serious state entanglement. Though Justice Brennan admitted that the judgment was "in tension" with earlier precedents,[42] he went on to hold that the narrow exemption was "state sponsorship of religious belief" regardless of the beneficiaries or uncompensated contributors.

As before, though even more vividly depicted, the Court was sharply divided in *Bullock*. Justice White, concurring, would have avoided the Establishment Clause entirely, premising invalidity on the Press Clause of the First Amendment. The content of the publication, he averred, determined exemption or nonexemption. It was the message carried that was conclusive and patently forbidden.[43] Justice Blackmun, joined by Justice O'Connor, agreed that a tax exemption limited to the sale of religious literature by religious groups violated the Establishment Clause. Yet he remained convinced that statutory rewriting might satisfy the three constitutional precepts at issue (Establishment, Free Exercise, and Press Clauses). Justice Blackmun suggested a tax exemption law that included not only religious writings but also philosophical literature emanating from nonreligious organizations. An adroit reconciliation of underlying values seemed to offer the key to a successful outcome.[44]

Justice Scalia, joined by Chief Justice Rehnquist and Justice Kennedy, submitted a trenchant dissent that, despite its rhetorical excesses, exposed many of the pitfalls that lay latent in this triadic enigma. He reminded his colleagues that accommodation often "slides over into promotion and neutrality into favoritism," but that the tax exemption statute under review was not "even a close case." If Justice Scalia's exposition went far toward diluting the Establishment Clause, he also revealed the inconsistencies in much of the Court's decision making in this area, from *Zorach v. Clauson* to *Corporation of the Presiding Bishop*. Accommodation, he noted pointedly, is unavoidably content-based and, if it is to be doctrinally viable, some adjustment of competing constitutional clauses must be made to assure meaningful harmony. Justice Scalia charged that *Bullock* had introduced a "new strain of irrationality" in the jurisprudence of the Religion Clauses. In closing, he complained that it was "not right" nor "constitutionally healthy" for the Court to assume that it was authorized to "refashion anew our civil society's relationship with religion."[45]

An uneasy epilogue to this line of disquieting and inconclusive cases came to pass in *Hernandez v. Commissioner of Internal Revenue*,[46] decided shortly after *Bullock*. A seven-member Court (with Justices Brennan and Kennedy not participating) sustained an IRS decision to hold nondeductible payments for auditing and training sessions conducted by a religious sect. Challenges premised on the Establishment and Free Exercise Clauses were rejected as unsubstantial and inapplicable. Justice Marshall, who wrote for the Court, was joined by Chief Justice Rehnquist and Justices White, Blackmun, and Stevens. The unusual coalition and the reasoning pursued reflected a studied avoidance of the critical issues and an effort, ostensibly effective, to sidestep the perilous terrain that lurked just beyond the borders delimited.

Justice Marshall, with little more than peripheral attention to the Religion Clauses, found that no unconstitutional denominational preference had been demonstrated; nor did he find any unwarranted differentiation among religious sects. The section of the Internal Revenue Code being contested, as Justice Marshall viewed it, met *Lemon's* three-pronged test. Of paramount concern, in the final analysis, was the nature of the payment—a remuneration for services or a "quid pro quo exchange," not a contribution or a gift.[47] To such an argument Justice O'Connor, joined in dissent by Justice Scalia, responded that the cases before the Court conveyed an "air of artificiality," an attempt to downplay constitutional difficulties, and an abjuration of responsibility to address serious issues by "converting a violation of the Establishment Clause into an 'administrative consistency argument' with an inadequate record."[48] Whether the dissenting opinion reflects accurately the motivations of the majority must remain conjectural, but Justice O'Connor's characterization seems to be a plausible one if not a precise or minutely unerring account of the Court's course. Surely it can be avouched with little danger of contravention that no advances in Establishment theory or doctrine emerged from *Hernandez*.[49]

If the search for a theory or principle of neutrality has resulted in a drift toward accommodation as an undulatory unifying motif, free exercise has not always gained commensurately in the process. An exception to the generally languid, if not negative, pattern lay in recent cases, implicating a sacrifice of employment tied to conscientious scruples, that may be traced to *Sherbert v. Verner*.[50] In *Sherbert*, a Sabbatarian had been denied unemployment compensation benefits predicated on the claimant's refusal to work on Saturdays and consequent failure to meet state requirements of availability for work. The Court, speaking through Justice Brennan, invoked the doctrine of unconstitutional conditions for the proposition that the receipt of public benefits might not be made contingent on a surrender of guaranteed constitutional rights. Nor had the state justified its action because of a "compelling" interest or the absence of an alternative way of achieving its purpose. Free exercise prevailed in *Sherbert*, but Justice Brennan's reasoning, in many respects, ran contrary to comparable decisions in the Sunday closing law cases.[51]

Sherbert controlled in succeeding cases extending through the 1980s. Initially, the Court reversed a state's denial of unemployment benefits to a religious adherent who had refused to produce armaments.[52] In like manner, a majority found in favor of a supervisory employee whose refusal to work on her Sabbath was premised on religious convictions and whose conversion occurred only after employment had begun.[53] Subsequently, but unlike the claimants in these cases, an applicant who lacked membership in an established sect or church sought benefits for declining to accept Sunday employment because, he said, as a Christian, he could not work on "the Lord's day."[54] Was there, in the circumstances, a violation of the Free Exercise Clause although the claimant's beliefs were not rooted in a specific tenet forbidding Sunday work? The Court, speaking through Justice White, rejected the notion that free exercise protection extended only to those "responding to the commands of a particular religious organization." So long as the refusal was premised on sincerely held religious beliefs and could not be regarded as "bizarre or incredible," free exercise claims were held to prevail in the absence of compelling state interests to the contrary.[55]

Apart from the employment context (limited and detached from other confounding factors), free exercise challenges have not succeeded with any degree of predictability. The practice of wearing religious headgear was not condoned as an acceptable exception from military regulations neutrally imposed. Chief Justice Rehnquist, writing for the Court, noted that uniform dress requirements were justified and ought to be accorded deferential treatment where, as here, military needs and the maintenance of discipline had to be served.[56] To like effect but in different circumstances, the Court rejected free exercise claims of devotional impediments advanced by prisoners. An even more deferential standard of review was in evidence than that applied to religious observances by members of the armed forces. A truncated test of reasonableness emerged, not requiring the state to confute the availability of alternatives.

A far more significant attenuation of *Sherbert* occurred in two cases, *Employment Division, Oregon Department of Human Resources v. Smith* (I and II),[57] arising from the use of peyote at a religious ceremony linked to the Native American Church. Counselors at a private drug and alcohol rehabilitation center, discharged for taking the drug, had been denied unemployment compensation benefits because, it was said, they had engaged in work-related misconduct. The Court, speaking through Justice Stevens in *Smith* I, admitted that rejection of the free exercise claim could not be sustained if the state supreme court's "unstated premise" was that the conduct was lawful in the state. For a determination whether the sacramental consumption of peyote was proscribed, the judgment was vacated and the case remanded to the state supreme court. It was the enigmatic message conveyed by the state court that led to a second review in *Smith* II. The state court found that peyote use violated the controlled substance statute, thus constituting a crime under state law for which no religiously inspired exception was provided. Yet, quizzically, the same court concluded that the prohibition was invalid under the First Amendment's Free Exercise Clause. Thus, the state was precluded from denying unemployment compensation to those whose discharge had resulted from ingestion of the drug. The state court's judicial legerdemain in the circumstances was a remarkable feat—an adroit resort to the federal Constitution by judges known for their reliance on state constitutional grounds for expansive interpretations of individual rights and liberties.

Justice Scalia, writing for the Supreme Court, denied that religious beliefs, no matter how resolutely or convincingly held and expressed, absolved an adherent from compliance with an "otherwise valid law prohibiting conduct that the State is free to regulate."[58] So long as the law was neutral and of general applicability, no constitutional infirmity resulted. The only exceptions to this rule affirming state action, Justice Scalia noted, lay in precedents combining and reinforcing free exercise concerns when conjoined with other First Amendment freedoms such as speech and press. Aside from a "hybrid situation," exemptions from general criminal laws need not be granted to those prompted by religiously oriented objectives. Justice Scalia rejected the so-called *Sherbert* test, the balancing of a burden on religious practices against counteractive compelling governmental interests, as inappropriate outside the area of unemployment compensation. To do otherwise, he noted, is to create a private right of individuals to disregard generally applicable laws, thereby leading to a "constitutional anomaly" contrary to "tradition and common sense."[59] Conditions akin to anarchy would result, Scalia warned, if persons could be relieved of civic obligations by the rigorous application of a compelling interest test to conduct premised on a plethora of religious preferences. An accommodation of religious beliefs and actions, where such a course is deemed desirable, ought to be accomplished through the political process even if religious practices not widely pursued might suffer. Such a consequence is preferable, Justice Scalia concluded, to a system in which "each conscience is a law unto itself or in which judges weigh the social importance of all laws against the centrality of all religious beliefs."[60]

Justice O'Connor, joined in part by Justices Brennan, Marshall, and Blackmun, took the Court's reasoning to be a departure from the mainstream of established free exercise jurisprudence. There was nothing "talismanic," she asserted, about generally applicable neutral laws or criminal prohibitions. She counseled case-by-case determinations to assure survival of the nation's historic commitment to religious liberty. To this end, a vigorously conceived compelling interest test was required, she implored, to protect an extant constitutional norm in a pluralistic society, clearly not the anomaly to which the Court referred. Justice O'Connor decried the Court's excessive reliance on majoritarianism which she found to be anathema to unpopular or newly emerging sects. Her sole reason for concurring in the Court's judgment was her agreement that the state had a compelling interest in regulating the use of peyote.[61] It was a difference of emphasis on the sufficiency and compelling nature of the state's regulatory interest that occasioned Justice Blackmun's dissent.[62]

What, then, has been the tenor and general purport of the meanings assigned to the Religion Clauses in a Court that has sought to project an image receptive to purveyors of religion and their adherents? Accommodation would seem to be the appropriate byword governing a complex set of formulas if, in fact, a relaxed, essentially positive view is to prevail. Yet a judicial willingness to sanction religious observances obliquely sponsored by or at least indirectly linked to the state has served largely to dilute the separation principle rather than to expand the scope of free exercise. The acceptable range of applicability has not extended beyond traditional religions and the conventional ceremonies, practices, and symbols associated with them. So-called "minority" religions and their "deviant" rites benefited little, if at all, from the Court's turn to accommodation and a course of indulgence pursued on a scale hitherto unknown.

The vitality of *Sherbert* as a precedent has been markedly reduced. Even in the limited area of unemployment benefits, it continues to exist more as a shell than as a viable and dependable conclusory force. State regulation of religious beliefs remains a significant and accepted rule when a generally applicable, otherwise valid, law is considered as a part of the decisional process. As in the past, the belief/action dichotomy continues to pose multiform questions. The status of free exercise as a preferred First Amendment freedom is not clear, and its future is increasingly dubious and precarious. Nor is the compelling interest test of any importance when the state acts under its police power to maintain order and to protect the social fabric. Selective exemptions, notably for practices considered sacrosanct or fundamental by "minority" religious groups, are not to be expected unless the Court finds the actions compatible with prevailing social mores, the burden on believers is not only substantial but inordinately onerous, and the conduct does not threaten vital concerns when, it appears, no presumptive protection obtains.

Free exercise, like establishment, has not achieved any measurable growth that places it in a distinctive category apart from or virtually immunized from a broad range of incursions resulting from the course of legislation. The level of scrutiny to be applied is not of a high order if, in fact, it ranks substantially above minimal review. Should the state invoke its police power, the means employed need not be limited to the narrowest measures required to attain the objective sought to be served. Thus encroachments on free exercise, akin to infringements on establishment safeguards, have been indulged to such an extent as to jeopardize the reach and impact of First Amendment liberties. Whether more blatantly invasive state activities will be permitted remains conjectural in a Court that seems to place an unusual emphasis on deference to governmental acts and an elusive majoritarianism even when the vigor of the Religion Clauses, as historically conceived, may be sacrificed.

NOTES

1. *See, e.g.*, Reynolds v. United States, 98 U.S. 145 (1879); Church of the Holy Trinity v. United States, 143 U.S. 226 (1892); Brodfield v. Roberts, 175 U.S. 291 (1899); United States v. Macintosh, 283 U.S. 605 (1931); Pierce v. Society of Sisters, 268 U.S. 510 (1925).

2. Zorach v. Clauson, 343 U.S. 306 (1952).

3. 310 U.S. 296 (1940).

4. 330 U.S. 1 (1947).

5. The flag-salute cases, perhaps the most compelling of this series of controversial decisions, interposed free expression into the Court's calculus of policy making. *See* Minersville School Dist. v. Gobitis, 310 U.S. 586 (1940) and West Virginia State Bd. of Educ. v. Barnette, 319 U.S. 624 (1943).

6. 330 U.S. at 18.

7. *Id.* at 49–60.

8. 333 U.S. 203 (1948).

9. *Id.* at 212–13, 231–32.

10. 343 U.S. 306 (1952).

11. McGowan v. Maryland, 336 U.S. 420 (1961).

12. Braunfeld v. Brown, 366 U.S. 599 (1961).

13. Engel v. Vitale, 370 U.S. 421 (1962); Abington School District v. Schempp, 374 U.S. 203 (1963).

14. Epperson v. Arkansas, 393 U.S. 97 (1968).

15. 403 U.S. 602 (1971).

16. 472 U.S. 38 (1985).

17. *Id.* at 68–69.

18. *Id.* at 110.

19. 482 U.S. 578 (1987).

20. 465 U.S. 668 (1984).

21. *Id.* at 692.

22. 492 U.S. 573 (1989).

23. *Id.* at 601.

24. *Id.* at 595.

25. *Id.* at 629–31.

26. *Id.* at 645.

27. *Id.* at 657, 663–64.

28. *Id.* at 604, 610.

29. 454 U.S. 263 (1981).

30. *Id.* at 274.

31. *Id.* at 276–77.
32. 98 Stat. 1302, U.S.C. §§ 4071–74.
33. 496 U.S. 226 (1990).
34. *Id.* at 250.
35. *Id.* at 260–61.
36. *Id.* at 269–70.
37. 483 U.S. 327 (1987).
38. *Id.* at 343–45.
39. *Id.* at 348.
40. 489 U.S. 1 (1989).
41. *Id.* at 18 n.8.
42. *See* Murdock v. Pennsylvania, 319 U.S. 105 (1943) and Follett v. McCormick, 321 U.S. 573 (1944).
43. 489 U.S. at 26.
44. *Id.* at 27–28.
45. *Id.* at 39–45.
46. 490 U.S. 680 (1989).
47. *Id.* at 695–98, 702–3.
48. *Id.* at 704, 712–13.
49. To like effect, a unanimous Court sustained a state's imposition of sales and use taxes on religious materials without finding any substantial incursions or violations of the Religion Clauses. Jimmy Swaggart Ministries v. Board of Equalization of Cal., 493 U.S. 378 (1990).
50. 374 U.S. 398 (1963).
51. *See* Braunfeld v. Brown, 366 U.S. 599 (1964) and Gallagher v. Crown Kosher Super Market, 366 U.S. 617 (1961).
52. Thomas v. Review Bd. of Ind. Employment Sec. Div., 450 U.S. 707 (1981).
53. Hobbie v. Unemployment Appeals Compensation Comm'n. of Fl., 480 U.S. 136 (1987).
54. Frazee v. Illinois Dept. of Employment Security, 489 U.S. 829 (1989).
55. *Id.* at 832–35, 834 n.2.
56. Goldman v. Weinberger, 475 U.S. 503 (1986).
57. 485 U.S. 660 (1988); 494 U.S. 872 (1990).
58. 494 U.S. at 878–79.
59. *Id.* at 885–86.
60. *Id.* at 890.
61. *Id.* at 901, 903–7.
62. *Id.* at 910–21.

Equal Protection, the Discrimination Barrier, and the Range of "Corrective" Remedies

Notions of equality, central to the American experience, have revealed anomalies as latter-day generations seek to redeem and to expand upon a legacy of promise reflected in the Declaration of Independence and kindred documents. From the close of the Civil War and the disillusionment of Reconstruction to the reawakening of national interest in civil rights causes in the late 1930s, little of a positive nature occurred to resolve the conflict between ideal and reality. The separate but equal formula, if not a constitutional standard in fact, had dominated the nation's equal protection jurisprudence since its adoption by the Supreme Court in *Plessy v. Ferguson*[1] during the closing decade of the nineteenth century.

It remained for the portentous decision in *Brown v. Board of Education*[2] to reverse practices of racial segregation that had pervaded and defiled the nation's heritage. The Court's early forays proved to be hazardous ventures for a judiciary[3] virtually unaided by Congress and the executive. Passage of the Civil Rights Act of 1964 and subsequent legislation, coupled with the establishment of a vast administrative mechanism, advanced egalitarianism more effectively during the span of a few decades than it had throughout most of the country's previous history. A new era of fulfillment seemed about to open, replete with efforts to bring to fruition what had just been hinted at as the basic structure of a proficient system of enforcement began to fall into place.

THE COURSE OF EDUCATIONAL DESEGREGATION

That the early steps to end segregation were not undertaken at the elementary and secondary school levels is not surprising. Too much was at stake in terms of the numbers involved and the dangers of disruption, if not of open violence, that might have resulted from efforts to undo hastily long-term, deeply felt antagonism against racial intermingling. As an interim measure, it appeared, institutions of higher education were selected strategically by the National Association for the Advancement of Colored People and eventually by the Court itself for the first engagements. In successive actions,[4] the Hughes Court, followed by the Vinson Court, insisted with ever-growing intensity that verifiably equal facilities be provided even if the *Plessy* formula was not directly overturned. Victories in the higher education cases, limited though they were, prepared the way for *Brown* and the hazardous road that lay beyond looking toward the elimination of segregation in the public schools, initially in the states of the Old Confederacy but eventually in other parts of the nation as well.

In the aftermath of *Brown*, questions related to the means of implementation arose with particular urgency in view of the resistance anticipated and the lack of support that could be expected from the other branches of the national government. The Court elected to place primary responsibility on the federal district courts to determine whether good-faith efforts were being undertaken by the local school districts involved. Courts were directed to retain jurisdiction of the cases during the ensuing period of transition. Throughout this period, judicial orders and decrees were to be entered to facilitate admissions to public schools on a racially nondiscriminatory basis "with all deliberate speed."[5] It was the latter phrase, derived from principles of equity, that came to be regarded as one of the salient keys to the process of desegregation. A series of cases reached the Supreme Court requiring a review of the guidelines necessary to maintain the momentum of desegregation. Challenges to court-ordered busing occurred frequently and, if somewhat reluctantly, the Court endorsed the device as a permissible remedy toward the elimination of "all vestiges" of state-imposed segregation.[6] But the Court stopped short of sanctioning interdistrict busing where suburban districts, especially in the north and west, had not been found to have fostered de jure practices. Housing patterns, it developed, had given rise to de facto segregation.[7] On the positive side, the Court shifted to the espousal of a "unitary" school system and, it was noted, the measure of "all deliberate speed" was "no longer constitutionally permissible."[8] Nonetheless, a majority steadfastly refused to set a date for completion of the desegregation process. Instead, incremental changes were instituted as the Court's pronouncements took on a more vigorous and emphatic tone toward the attainment of full-scale integration. The Court even sustained the power of a federal judge to require a school board to raise taxes to provide funds for a "magnet" plan intended to achieve integration.[9]

With the passage of several decades since the *Brown* ruling, federal courts have been called upon to offer guidance concerning conditions that might lead to an end of judicial supervision in the hundreds of school districts affected. The Supreme Court, in *Board of Education of Oklahoma City Public Schools v. Dowell*,[10] entered upon one of its most detailed discourses on the subject—doubtless prepared as an effort to suggest an impending close to an era of turmoil and attention to trying problems of implementation. Chief Justice Rehnquist, who wrote for the majority, reminded observers that federal supervision was never intended to be more than a temporary measure to remedy past discrimination. School districts, he contended, were not to be condemned to "judicial tutelage" for the indefinite future. The commands of equal protection did not so require. Instead, district courts were to consider whether good faith compliance had occurred and whether the "vestiges of de jure segregation had been eliminated as far as practicable." The decrees issued, Chief Justice Rehnquist asserted, were not intended to operate in perpetuity but only for a "reasonable period" to rectify constitutional violations.[11]

Justice Marshall, joined in dissent by Justices Blackmun and Stevens, took issue with what he apparently took to be the Court's facile approach to the lifting of the desegregation decree in question. He argued that central to the standard for dissolution should be an evaluation of the extent to which "the stigmatic injury associated with segregated schools" no longer persists. To the majority's stress on the desirability of a return to local control, Justice Marshall responded with words of caution that the interests of Afro-American children ought not to be sacrificed in the process. He emphasized that, to achieve "make whole" relief, redress must be afforded for any effects attributable to de jure segregation even if continued enforcement of segregation no long obtains.[12]

The following year, in *Freeman v. Pitts*,[13] the Court continued to redefine the stages of judicial withdrawal and the conditions that warranted successive steps in the return of a district to local control. The "unitariness" concept, Justice Kennedy noted for the Court, has neither fixed meaning nor content and does not restrict a court's discretion in a way that "departs from equitable principles." It is the inherent flexibility of equity that is intended to ensure an orderly removal of judicial supervision. Relinquishment by means of incremental phases, Justice Kennedy pointed out, does not require full compliance in every area of school operations. So long as a "good-faith commitment to a constitutional course of action has been demonstrated," a formula of gradualism may mark the final stages of desegregation while assuring that the vestiges of past discrimination have been eliminated to a practicable extent.[14]

Retention of judicial control grows less consequential, the Court observed in *Freeman*, as the de jure violation becomes increasingly remote in time and demographic changes intrude, altering the racial composition of the school population. "Heroic measures" are not required when external factors such as changing residential patterns are responsible for racial imbalance. Justice Kennedy held that the "causal link between current conditions and the prior violation is even more attenuated if the school district has demonstrated its good faith."[15] Even more pointedly, Justice Scalia, concurring, maintained that the constitutional right at issue was "equal racial access to schools, not access to racially equal schools."[16] He predicted a reversion to conventional principles of law and a return to locally controlled schools with pupils permitted to attend schools closest to their homes.[17]

With the retirement of Justice Marshall in 1991, a near-unanimous Court has signaled in *Freeman* that, while it remains concerned about remedying the effects of vestiges of past state-imposed segregation, a far less assertive pattern is likely to emerge. The so-called *Green* factors[18] designed to effectuate a unitary system, the notion of continuing judicial supervision of school districts, an "affirmative duty" to desegregate, and like corrective measures have begun to fade into obscurity as remnants of a bygone age. Perhaps, despite Justice Scalia's audacious bluntness, he may have spoken for what his colleagues less candidly left unsaid. Scalia considered "absurd" any assumption that violations dating from the 1960s or earlier would have any "appreciable effect" on current school operations.[19] Whether this prediction will come to pass, even as hundreds of federal courts throughout the nation retain jurisdiction over suspect school systems, remains an open question. Henceforth, it appears, a presumptively negative or querulous inquiry is less likely to characterize judicial review of school systems no longer prodded by what formerly was a searching constitutional imperative.

THE AFFIRMATIVE ACTION, "REVERSE" DISCRIMINATION IMBROGLIO

Equal protection, in its least sophisticated form, connotes an artless sense of equality and a Constitution that, in the words of the first Justice Harlan, can only be looked upon as color-blind.[20] If, more realistically, the law has never been color-blind in nondiscriminatory terms, race needs to be taken into account as a significant element, at least on an interim basis, in combatting racism and in making amends for past acts of intolerance. From the mid-1960s onward, governments at several levels have opted, in varying degrees, for affirmative action programs to recruit blacks, women, and other minority persons to encourage their entry into the American mainstream. But it is not aggressive recruiting that has led to major conflict and dissension even among civil rights advocates. Quotas and preferential hiring and promotion practices, critics contend, have disadvantaged members of all groups since the overt emphasis on race-consciousness stigmatizes rather than benefits those affected. By contrast, defenders of intensive affirmative action measures insist that such programs are the only available means of correcting past injustices and of substantially advancing the fortunes of disaffected minorities.

How, then, has this dilemma been resolved within the bounds of a Constitution that, with the exception of the Fourteenth Amendment, offers no basis for a resort, statutory or otherwise, to avant garde, unprecedented doctrines of egalitarianism? The Court's initial response was an evasive one that postponed a decision without any hint of the formidable issues that the Justices ineluctably had to confront.[21] Subsequent cases could not avoid the substantive issues, but the early results were inconclusive.[22]

A decidedly mixed pattern began to emerge. A minority "set-aside" measure was upheld[23] while violations of employee seniority rights were held to be prohibited on constitutional and statutory grounds.[24] Hiring and promotion goals, little more than euphemistic labels for quotas, were permitted to take effect in the early years of the Rehnquist Court.[25] As recent appointees began to exercise effective influence, a negative note was struck in *City of Richmond v. J.A. Croson Co.*[26] The Court, speaking through Justice O'Connor, distinguished a national program where Congress utilized its enforcement powers under the fifth section of the Fourteenth Amendment from the constraints imposed upon the states under Section 1. The latter, a majority averred, was narrowly drawn to require specificity in identifying the source of the discrimination and demonstration of a compelling interest in allotting public contracts on the basis of race. Thus "remedial relief," when resorted to, had to be premised on a strict scrutiny test necessitating that any program be "narrowly tailored" to remedy the effects of prior discrimination. Findings must assure citizens that, as Justice

O'Connor viewed it, any deviation from equal treatment was a temporary measure "taken in the service of the goal of equality itself."[27] In dissent, Justice Marshall, joined by Justices Brennan and Blackmun, termed the decision in the Richmond case a "grape-shot attack" on race-conscious remedies and its reliance on strict scrutiny an "unwelcome development" founded on a resort to a "daunting" standard. Consequently, as Marshall perceived it, the Court's affirmative action jurisprudence had suffered a "deliberate and giant step backward"—one that sounded a "full-scale retreat" from race-conscious efforts.[28]

Like school desegregation, affirmative action proceedings, measured in terms of reverse or benign discrimination, seem to have reached their apex with less exacting requirements apparent in the offing. A return to strict scrutiny as the criterion of validity augurs a period of moderation, if not of cessation, in the development of programs explicitly designed to assist minorities. Legislative acts and executive directives may continue to provide set-aside designations and comparable devices. But the momentum for aggressive implementation has subsided and, lacking convincing judicial support, it is not likely that the programs will expand or even flourish profusely over the long term. Instead, there are indications that equal protection will revert to more conventional channels—protective of citizen rights generally but no longer so overtly preferential to specified groups as to be open to charges of disfavoring others in society. The constitutional debate doubtless will resume and be spirited at times though a sense of urgency and the earlier stimulus to militant intervention are missing.

GENDER-BASED DIFFERENCES, AGE DISCRIMINATION, AND STATUTORY FORMULAS

For a century following adoption of the Fourteenth Amendment, the plight of women, as a discrete group, was never seriously considered by reference to safeguards provided by the equal protection clause. It is not mere coincidence that the Court's first major gender-related venture[29] coincided with congressional attention to a proposed equal rights amendment and a review of the issues raised throughout the nation. Despite much wrangling regarding the level of scrutiny to be applied, the Court fell short of a majority to place gender issues in a suspect category.[30]

The most that has been sustained is an intermediate level that prompts "heightened" review. This has proved to be a requirement ranging between interpretive poles—a status that calls for greater justification in support of state action than minimal rationality prescribes but that never reaches a point of strict scrutiny shifting the onus of responsibility to the state.[31] Among the most telling cases was *Orr v. Orr*,[32] a decision that introduced unisex elements into the domestic relations equation as it made wives as well as husbands liable for the payment of alimony in the wake of a divorce. But nowhere in the Supreme Court's many pronouncements is there any enhanced support for strict scrutiny as a standard of review. Such scrutiny, it appears, requires adoption of an equal rights amendment to the Constitution, a measure incorporated in a number of state constitutions though not in the national charter.

To a far greater extent than challenges premised on constitutional mandates or inferences attributed to them, gender-related cases are grounded in statutes or administrative regulations. A section of the Civil Rights Act of 1964, taken in concert with amendments drawn from the Pregnancy Discrimination Act of 1978, was cited to preclude an employer's "fetal protection" policy which, it was charged, had discriminatory effects on women. As a majority construed the provisions in question,[33] the exclusion of females with childbearing capacity from lead-exposed jobs constituted sex discrimination. The classification, predicated on the basis of a potential for pregnancy, involved disparate treatment singling out women in a way that had no application to male employees.

That the company undertook the exclusion for presumably beneficent reasons, that is, to safeguard future offspring from harm, did not transform the policy into a facially neutral one.[34] Justice Blackmun, for the Court, noted that the "safety exception" is restricted to a job-related inability to perform. Women "as capable of doing their jobs as their male counterparts" may not be required to make choices between a job and childbearing.[35] Decisions concerning future generations do not justify sex-specific fetal-protection policies best left to parents who conceive and ultimately raise children rather than to employers. Nor did the possibility that tort liability might result prove to be persuasive, Justice Blackmun declared, and establish a bona fide occupational qualification (BFOQ) under the Civil Rights Act. Should this occur, federal preemption might come into play to preclude state intervention.[36]

To the contrary, Justice White, joined in a concurrence by Chief Justice Rehnquist and Justice Kennedy, was not prepared to dismiss cavalierly the possibility that causes of action for prenatal injuries might come to pass. He did not perceive as necessarily probable a preemptive holding to prevent the application of such state common law remedies. And Justice White was not convinced that the Court's "cramped reading" of the BFOQ defense reflected congressional intent, in effect, to disregard public safety interests.[37] Justice Scalia, concurring, was less apprehensive than Justice White that any action required would give rise to state tort law liability. Nevertheless, he declined to join the Court in suggesting that increased employer costs alone could not support a BFOQ defense.[38]

A monetary damages remedy, denied to a victim of sex discrimination in the federal courts, was sustained by the Supreme Court in an expansive construction of a series of education and civil rights law amendments.[39] Justice White, writing for the Court, inferred a right to appropriate relief because, he argued, Congress had not sought to abandon the "traditional presumption" in favor of all available remedies in a suit brought to enforce a federal statute.[40] A majority undertook an arcane exercise in statutory construction in support of the distinction between a cause of action and a remedy. Award of the latter, Justice White stated, did not increase judicial power, and so no violation of the doctrine of separation of powers might properly be claimed. Indeed, White asserted, a court's failure to provide relief in the circumstances might remove significant safeguards against legislative and executive abuses of power and threaten to undermine the independence of the judiciary.[41] Once again Justice Scalia concurred though he reminded his colleagues that when, as here, rights of action are judicially implied, "categorical limitations upon their remedial scope may be judicially implied as well."[42]

Like gender-related cases, age discrimination controversies often turn on statutory interpretation rather than equal protection principles. In fact, the intermediate level of scrutiny applicable to challenges predicated on sexual bias does not pertain to disputes linked to age discrimination. The Court has had ample opportunities to embrace age within its self-styled category of suspect classifications or at least to subject it to heightened scrutiny. Yet, whenever the occasion has arisen, a majority has declined to do so. Perhaps the Court came closest to a reasoned explanation when, in *Gregory v. Ashcroft*,[43] it dealt with charges that the mandatory retirement of state judges was contrary to the Fourteenth Amendment's equal protection clause. Justice O'Connor, writing for the Court, found that no more than a rational basis test need be applied. Age, she noted pointedly, was not a suspect classification; nor could a fundamental interest in public employment be advanced in assessing the removal of judges who had reached the age of 70.[44]

Moving to elaborate upon and to reinforce the principles set out, Justice O'Connor went on to describe the threat of physical deterioration of judges at age 70, inadequate mechanisms for performance review, and a "legitimate, indeed compelling" public interest in a judiciary capable of carrying out demanding tasks and responsibilities. She sought to demonstrate that judges generally lacked public accountability and, therefore, that their work had to be appraised by standards not appropriate for other state employees whose performance was more readily discernible and whose possible removal from office was more easily accomplished. All the same, Justice O'Connor conceded that mandatory retirement was premised on a generalization that "may not be true at all."[45] Had the Court not elected to utilize an exceedingly permissive level of rational basis analysis, the equal protection challenge could not have been so cavalierly dismissed as a valid constitutional encumbrance.

It is noteworthy that the separate opinions in *Gregory* barely touched upon the equal protection issue. Justice White, joined by Justice Stevens, dealt only cursorily with the question, expressing no more than agreement with the majority's treatment.[46] Moreover, Justice Blackmun, in dissent with Justice Marshall, stated by way of a concluding footnote that the argument need not be considered since, in his view, a statutory violation had occurred and controlled the outcome. In fact, the crux of the divisions lay in the construction of provisions of the Federal Age Discrimination in Employment Act, that is, in the language regarding the status of judges as "employees" or policymakers. Constitutional considerations, it seemed, were to be shunted aside no matter how compellingly presented and though they had previously been subjected to evasive techniques.

It has become increasingly evident that further movement toward the adoption of any level of heightened scrutiny is unlikely to occur with respect to age- or gender-related discrimination. The former appears to be fixed at a rational basis stage while the latter continues to rest on a decisional plateau linked to intermediate review. Little growth or decline is to be expected for the foreseeable future or at least as long as the Rehnquist Court remains an operative entity. Failure of the Equal Rights Amendment appears to have had a decisive effect upon the Justices. The revival of prospects for substantial change is dependent upon a renewal of congressional interest in the amendment or its equivalent. An enhanced constitutional predicate applicable to age discrimination is even less probable. The composition of the Court suggests that growth patterns are static. Any designation of additional categories, premised on departures from conventional review, should not be anticipated.

Of overriding significance for advocates are developments in the legislative-executive forum. The making of policy and the introduction of innovative remedies largely result from political considerations related to but not necessarily paralleling the course of constitutional decision making. For example, the Civil Rights Act of 1991,[47] in part, was intended to provide statutory correctives to combat harassment in the workplace and to codify such vague, judicially contrived terms as "job related."[48] Whether Congress can be relied upon to supply amplified remedies or to offer definitional precision or linguistic enlargement remains problematic.

An unexpected avenue of decision making reopened at the close of the Court's term in the early summer of 1992. Often overlooked, if not forgotten, in view of the impressive attention afforded desegregation in the public schools has been higher education—derivatively the area that initially gave rise to cases in the elementary and secondary schools. In *United States v. Fordice*,[49] the Court, with Justice Scalia casting the sole dissenting vote, remanded for review of "constitutionally suspect" practices a Mississippi case involving remnants of segregation persisting in the state college system. Justice White's opinion for the majority posed anew questions that ranged beyond a policy of professed equal access. Nonetheless, fears have been expressed that more rigorous enforcement of egalitarian norms may have an adverse and perhaps a fatally ruinous impact upon the future of black colleges. A return to an activist constitutionalism, it appears, may prove to be more detrimental than helpful to the realization of long-sought goals in this initiatory, oft-heralded arena of the civil rights struggle.

NOTES

1. 163 U.S. 537 (1896).
2. 347 U.S. 483 (1954).
3. *See, e.g.*, Cooper v. Aaron, 358 U.S. 1 (1958).
4. Missouri ex rel. Gaines v. Canada, 305 U.S. 337 (1938); Sweatt v. Painter, 339 U.S. 629 (1950); McLaurin v. Oklahoma State Regents, 339 U.S. 637 (1950).
5. Brown v. Board of Educ., 349 U.S. 294 (1955).
6. Swann v. Charlotte-Mecklenberg Bd. of Educ., 402 U.S.1 (1971).
7. Milliken v. Bradley, 418 U.S. 717 (1974).
8. Alexander v. Holmes County Bd. of Educ., 396 U.S. 19 (1969).
9. Missouri v. Jenkins, 495 U.S. 33 (1990).
10. 112 L. Ed. 2d 715 (1991).
11. *Id.* at 728–30.
12. *Id.* at 734–36, 741.
13. 118 L. Ed. 2d 108 (1992).
14. *Id.* at 132–35.
15. *Id.* at 137–38.
16. *Id.* at 142.
17. *Id.* at 144.
18. *See* Green v. New Kent County School Bd., 391 U.S. 430 (1968).
19. 118 L. Ed. 2d at 144.

20. 163 U.S. at 559 (Harlan, J. dissenting).

21. DeFunis v. Odegaard, 416 U.S. 312 (1974).

22. *See* Regents of the University of California v. Bakke, 438 U.S. 265 (1978). Charges of reverse discrimination had been made by a white male medical school applicant. A fragmented Court narrowly sustained affirmative action programs, but not quota systems.

23. Fullilove v. Klutznick, 448 U.S. 448 (1980). *Cf.* United Steelworkers of Am. v. Weber, 443 U.S. 193 (1979).

24. Firefighters' Local Union No. 1784 v. Stotts, 467 U.S. 561 (1984); Wygant v. Jackson Bd. of Educ., 476 U.S. 267 (1986).

25. United States v. Paradise, 480 U.S. 149 (1987); Johnson v. Transportation Agency, 480 U.S. 616 (1987).

26. 488 U.S. 469 (1989).

27. *Id.* at 490, 499, 505–10.

28. *Id.* at 529, 555, 561. In Metro Broadcasting, Inc. v. Federal Communications Comm'n., 111 L. Ed. 2d 445 (1990), a narrow majority, led by Justice Brennan, maintained the federal-state Fourteenth Amendment distinction and sustained a preferential program for minorities in the award of broadcast licenses.

29. Reed v. Reed, 404 U.S. 71 (1971).

30. Frontiero v. Richardson, 411 U.S. 677 (1973).

31. *See* Craig v. Boren, 429 U.S. 190 (1976) for the development of principles that remain controlling. *Cf.* Mississippi Univ. for Women v. Hogan, 458 U.S. 718 (1982); Rostker v. Goldberg, 453 U.S. 57 (1981); Michael M. v. Superior Court, 450 U.S. 464 (1981).

32. Orr v. Orr, 440 U.S. 268 (1979).

33. United Automobile Workers v. Johnson Controls, Inc., 113 L. Ed. 2d 158 (1991).

34. *Id.* at 173–74.

35. *Id.* at 177.

36. *Id.* at 178–80.

37. *Id.* at 182–86.

38. *Id.* at 189.

39. Franklin v. Gwinnett County Public Schools, 117 L. Ed. 2d 208 (1992).

40. *Id.* at 221.

41. *Id.* at 220–22.

42. *Id.* at 224.

43. 115 L. Ed. 2d 410 (1991).

44. *Id.* at 430.

45. *Id.* at 431–32.

46. *Id.* at 432.

47. 105 Stat. 1071, amendments to 42 U.S.C. 1981 *et al.*

48. *See, e.g.*, Wards Cove Packing Co., Inc. v. Atonio, 490 U.S. 642 (1989).

49. 120 L. Ed .2d 575 (1992).

———————— 7 ————————

Aspects of the Criminal Law: Reversals of Course and the Mutability of Precedents

Among the controversial legacies of the Warren years was a plethora of cases touching upon the criminal law of the states, eventually transforming constitutionally derived safeguards into what was, in effect, a judicially prescribed code of criminal procedure. This dramatic conversion substantially altered traditional norms in a federal system that had previously posited a major, if not an exclusive, role for the states in the elucidation and application of the criminal law. In large measure, the alterations introduced paralleled more broadly based developments stemming from the "nationalization" of the Bill of Rights. A persistent centripetal course prevailed—one hitherto unknown in the annals of the criminal law or, more generally, in relation to a Bill of Rights historically intended to prevent national not state intrusions upon individual liberties. The operative catalyst lay in the Fourteenth Amendment's Due Process Clause, a conduit for the absorption or incorporation of segments of the Bill of Rights that facilitated their applicability to state proceedings.

If any case became the symbol and, more often, the target of critics of Warren Court activism it was *Miranda v. Arizona*,[1] the product of spirited decision making that Justice Harlan characterized as the Court's "new constitutional code of rules for confessions." The extension of the Fifth Amendment's privilege against self-incrimination to custodial police interrogations contained more explicit directions than any previously announced; but the ground rules, though specified at length, were not so excessive as to cast existing investigative procedures into disarray. Yet the *"Miranda* warnings," as they came to be known (frequently in derision), served to fuel attacks upon the Court, generally attributed to proponents of a vigorous regimen of criminal law enforcement. Even when *Miranda* and the cases associated with it came to the Supreme Court and before judgment was rendered, the attorneys general of more than half the states and representatives of a national district attorneys' association had joined in the filing of briefs. Outcries against *Miranda* and its much-feared aftermath extended well beyond the judicial system as a salient feature of the Court's fulfilled agenda—a feature said to threaten a social order premised, at least in part, on effective law enforcement.

That the Warren Court's criminal law cases were far more varied than *Miranda*, perhaps more compelling and arguably as novel in their impact, was lost upon many court observers, much less the lay public and legislators. A major turnabout occurred in *Mapp v. Ohio*[2] when the exclusionary rule was held to be enforceable against the states. The rule, an oft-decried buttress of Fourth Amendment jurisprudence, precluded use of evidence secured by means of an unlawful seizure. Whether the exclusionary rule is intended to deter police misconduct, to ensure the integrity of the judiciary, or to govern for sundry other reasons, it has been the subject of contentious debate and policy making almost since its inception.[3] Few issues so rankled the Burger Court, especially the chief justice, as much as the exclusionary rule though its abandonment was not seriously proposed for want of a meaningful alternative.[4] Perhaps the Burger Court's most telling incursion upon the rule lay in its adoption of the good-faith exception, thus permitting inclusion of evidence seized by means of a warrant issued without probable cause if good-faith reliance on the defective warrant could be demonstrated.[5]

A further sampling of Warren Court precedents in relation to the criminal law,[6] while indicative of judicial activism and a growing tendency to "rein in" state prosecutorial excesses, did not lead to widespread public tirades. Nor did the Burger Court engage in a major reformulation of state criminal procedures on a scale reflective of repeated predications that a significant diminution of safeguards was likely to ensue. Instead, the Burger years projected the image of a Court almost perpetually in a transitional state although with less positive attributes, extended by judicial fiat, than previously envisioned or realized. If some Warren Court precedents were undermined, the results were not decidedly negative when measured against the existing corpus of the criminal law. The most substantial assaults occurred with respect to *Miranda* and its progeny and, even with respect to this limited array, the results were sporadic and cyclical in their impact.[7]

The Rehnquist Court, by contrast, moved decisively to rework a wide array of judicially devised components of the criminal law by directly overturning or materially eroding their value as precedents. Noticeably missing was any effort to pursue a course of moderation and restraint which had served to guide many Burger Court decisions in an era when adherence to the doctrine of stare decisis generally prevailed. During the spring of 1991, the Rehnquist Court's turn away from established precedents took on a momentum of its own as the development of the criminal law began to reflect an activist impetus at variance with the gradualism of previous years. A new majority seemed determined to "reach out" for cases that might be used as vehicles to introduce revisionist formulations. The intent was unmistakable—to undo a cluster of safeguards hitherto regarded as abiding features of the constitutional order.

A long-lived postulate characteristic of the American system of criminal justice recognizes the preservation of fairness in the trial process as a basic tenet more fundamental than the truth-seeking function itself. The integrity and sanctity of a fair trial have long been assured by constitutional guarantees of due process. Of the protective measures provided the defendant, few exceed in depth and persuasiveness the warrant that the products of coerced confessions will not be permitted to be considered at trial. It has been held to be axiomatic that a conviction founded upon an involuntary confession cannot be sustained regardless of the confession's truth or falsity or of the availability of other evidence that might support a conviction.[8] The resulting judgment is vitiated as violative of Fifth or Fourteenth Amendment due process.[9]

In *Arizona v. Fulminante*,[10] the accused had made a confession, implicating himself as a child murderer, to a paid government informant out of fear of inmate physical violence in a federal prison to which he had been committed. The state supreme court initially affirmed his conviction of murder and the death sentence imposed by the trial court but, on a motion for reconsideration, the conviction was reversed and a retrial ordered because the confession had been coerced. The state appealed to the federal Supreme Court which affirmed the judgment below amid a welter of opinions by different majorities and individual Justices for a confusing set of holdings in many respects akin to seriatim decision making. For disparate reasons and, in each instance, by the narrowest of margins, the Court concluded that the confession in question had been coerced, that it was subject to harmless-error analysis, but that it was not harmless as applied to this conviction.

The crux of the differences lay in the applicability of less demanding harmless-error review to the admission at trial of a coerced confession. In a departure from precedent, Chief Justice Rehnquist held that harmless-error analysis sufficed in regard to an involuntary confession since no more than a trial error was at issue. He distinguished such a category of "errors" from "structural defects in the constitution of the trial mechanism, which defy analysis by 'harmless-error' standards."[11] The latter were said to include deprivations of the right to counsel, of the right to a public trial, of a trial before an impartial judge, and of a grand jury based upon exclusions of persons of the defendant's race.

To Justice White, joined by Justices Marshall, Blackmun, and Stevens, prevailing precedents did not sanction application of the harmless-error rule to coerced confessions. The latter, Justice White argued, was intrinsically different from the ordinary series of trial errors to which Rehnquist had referred. A confession was said to be so basic to a fair trial that infractions could never be looked upon as harmless. It was, Justice White averred, "fundamentally different from other types of erroneously admitted evidence."[12] To this end, he noted that a defendant's confession can be the most probative and damaging evidence admitted against him. In an accusatorial system, Justice White stressed, the state must establish guilt apart from coerced words of the accused. To do otherwise runs contrary to established mores and conventions that distinguish accepted criminal justice procedures from those associated with a much-condemned inquisitorial system.[13]

Apart from proscriptions of such practices as coerced confessions and positive safeguards emanating from the Fifth and Sixth Amendments, provision for access to remedial processes for persons restrained of liberty ranks high among the rights guaranteed the accused in the Anglo-American system. Petitions of state prisoners for collateral review by way of writs of habeas corpus have been authorized by Congress since 1867. Common law procedures were expanded and, in part, superseded at the time to ensure adequate enforcement of the Reconstruction Acts. But it was the extension of the writ's availability to prisoners in state custody that distinguished the 1867 statute and that inaugurated a plethora of cases and amending legislation. The flow of petitions that ensued, frequently baseless and even spurious, led to the formulation of what came to be known as the doctrine of abuse of the writ. A recent examination of the doctrine, and perhaps its most extensive and critical assessment, arose in *McCleskey v. Zant*,[14] among the cluster of criminal law cases decided in the spring of 1991. It was here that the Supreme Court defined the doctrine, in succinct fashion, as a "complex and evolving body of equitable principles informed and controlled by historical usage, statutory developments, and judicial decisions."[15]

What persuaded the Court to enter upon a major inquiry into resorts to the Great Writ and the threshold considerations that came into play? While it has often been said that habeas petitions may not substitute for appropriate appeals, the scope of contemporary review under the writ has ranged well beyond minimal issues of jurisdiction. The number of petitions filed by state prisoners has

risen sharply. Although the percentage of successful efforts continues to be low, recurring and vexing questions of federalism and
comity persist and are difficult to treat in an atmosphere charged
with resentment by state courts and judges. Federal intrusion has
been looked upon as a threat to state autonomy in the articulation
of the criminal law. In addition, the promotion of disrespect for the
finality of convictions has opened the way to new trials that prejudice the government's case because of memory lapses and the
continuing dispersion of witnesses as the time interval between the
initial trial and a possible retrial widens. What is more, it is claimed,
meritorious applications have been submerged by worthless ones
spawned by inmates who imperil the effectuation of longstanding
safeguards and rights by making a mockery of the writ and due
process predicated on senseless illusions defaming trial judges and
prosecutors.

The majority's response to such allegations in *McCleskey* was
forceful and unrelenting—so much so as to place in jeopardy the
continued viability of the writ as a basis of redress in state criminal
cases. Justice Kennedy, writing for the Court, substantially modified long-term precedents, announcing an exacting "cause and
prejudice" standard that established a strict-liability test for state
prisoners seeking to avail themselves of habeas corpus relief. The
revised abuse-of-the-writ doctrine required that, for a successive
petition to prevail, there be demonstrated the existence of "objective factors that constitute cause" for failure to raise a claim in an
earlier petition or, in the alternative, that a fundamental miscarriage
of justice might otherwise result. In support of the new standard,
Justice Kennedy claimed its acknowledgment of the "historic purpose and function of the writ."[16]

In dissent, Justice Marshall, joined by Justices Blackmun and
Stevens, denounced the Court's departure from established precedents and principles defining the abuse-of-the-writ doctrine. The
new test, Justice Marshall asserted, was both unwise and unfair, a
product of untoward judicial activism motivated by disregard of
judicial and statutory norms and of considerations of liberty intended to be protected. Substitution of a new rule of cause and
prejudice for the less intrusive good-faith "deliberate abandon-

ment" standard that previously prevailed was said to be an "unjustifiable assault" on the writ and a way of rewarding "state misconduct and deceit." The dissent also charged that the Court had sought to interject by judicial fiat what Congress had rejected in the course of its most recent revision of the basic habeas corpus statute. To have done so, Justice Marshall averred, violated the generally accepted rule that the Court is not to function as a "backup legislature for the reconsideration of failed attempts to amend existing statutes."[17]

A divided Court, beset by intemperate, emotional opinions, revealed traces of the melodrama that had characterized previous judicial interludes when clashes were intense and prolonged. That like upheavals have occurred during periods of major adjustment and importunate change is indicative of the turnabout in criminal law proceedings. It is difficult to attribute the heated exchanges in *McCleskey* merely to differences in perceptions of abuses in applications for the writ of habeas corpus. The ease or stringency of state prisoner access to the appellate courts is symptomatic of broader currents touching upon the rights of the accused. The Rehnquist Court, it seems, has embarked upon a studied, intentional course less attentive to broadening or substantially preserving constitutional safeguards long associated with the process of the criminal law. The alterations undertaken are far more expansive than a strict adherence to the state exhaustion doctrine before federal remedies can be sought or an insistence upon a rigorous regard for procedural and sequential orderliness in the framing of claims advanced to merit issuance of the writ. Nor do considerations of federalism appear to be of paramount importance notwithstanding the resentment of state judges to federal intervention—a constant complaint that remains as compelling and persistent as it always has been.[18]

If restraints upon the availability of the Great Writ and the adoption of relaxed standards relating to the admissibility of coerced confessions have been primary indicators of a major reversal of course, other examples of changing attitudes have also become evident. Fourth Amendment rights, long objects of controversy and travail in the evolution of the criminal law, have been further eroded in a Court inclined to read the rights of the accused in austere and unsympathetically literal terms. Searches conducted by police officers in public places have often raised issues of coercive intent and Fourth Amendment values. That persons can be approached and questioned in open lobbies and terminals and requested to provide voluntary consent to the search of their luggage is not in dispute. But the dilemma has remained, does a like rule apply where officers are "working the buses" in their effort to interdict drug sales and distribution? The Supreme Court of Florida found the interior of the bus sufficiently confining so that police encounters were held to be intimidating and restrictive of the suspect's freedom of movement. It adopted a rule that, in effect, made random bus searches unconstitutional.

The federal Supreme Court, in *Florida v. Bostick*,[19] reversed the state court's determination, premised on a finding that a consensual encounter had, in fact, occurred, thereby not causing the inquiry to rise to the level of a possible incursion upon Fourth Amendment interests. Without deciding whether or not a seizure had taken place, Justice O'Connor, writing for the majority, declined to single out buses as notably coercive environments meriting exacting constitutional scrutiny. Instead, she noted, practices arguably distasteful could not be proscribed so long as cooperation remained voluntary. Justice Marshall, joined in dissent by Justices Blackmun and Stevens, took exception to what he described as the "suspicionless police sweep of buses." He depicted the "dragnet" style actions as incompatible with practices representative of a free society and as more closely associated with the tyranny of totalitarian states. The majority's reasoning, Justice Marshall asserted, bordered on sophism and "trivialize[d]" the values that underlay the Fourth Amendment.[20]

Perhaps minimally less dramatic but no less indicative of a continuing Fourth Amendment retreat were a series of cases that reflected departures more conventionally linked to contemporary doctrines of search and seizure. With reference to the "automobile exception" to the Fourth Amendment's warrant requirement, the Court reconsidered and set aside separate categorizations in favor of a single rule governing automobile searches. In *California v. Acevedo*,[21] Justice Blackmun, for the majority, sustained the validity of a warrantless search of containers in a vehicle when, in earlier cases, the search of the entire car would have been necessary if and when probable cause had been established. This effort to provide doctrinal symmetry, Blackmun maintained, would have little detrimental effect upon privacy interests. Instead, he contended, the new rule would eliminate the confusion that impeded effective law enforcement. Justice Stevens, joined in dissent by Justice Marshall and in large measure by Justice White, denounced the majority's holding and particularly its rationale as an "insufficient" basis for the creation of a new exception to the warrant requirement. He prophesied that the Court had become a "loyal foot soldier" in the war against crime notwithstanding the loss of liberty incurred as a result.[22]

In cases predating the Warren Court as well as in others significantly influenced by prevailing trends of the era itself[23] were oft-repeated efforts to define "seizure" of a person within the meaning of the Fourth Amendment. The common law of arrest required that an animate or inanimate object be brought within physical control or "possessed" before seizure could be said to have occurred. But, the question remained, did the common law control the meaning of the Fourth Amendment or did seizure take on a more expansive connotation when viewed as a constitutional precept? If the precedents remained somewhat ambiguous concerning the latter, the Court's opinion in *California v. Hodari D.*[24] moved the law strikingly closer to the earlier narrow confines of the common law. Even if, as Justice Scalia assumed for the majority, pursuit of the suspect by the police had constituted a "show of authority," no seizure had occurred; the narcotics abandoned in the course of the chase had not been the fruit of a seizure or attempted arrest and, therefore, they were not properly excludable at trial.

Justice Stevens, dissenting with Justice Marshall, took the majority to task for adopting a definition of seizure that was "profoundly unwise." To Stevens, the "touchstone" of a seizure lay in restraint of an individual's liberty whether effected by way of a physical grasp or stop or, more subtly, by a show of force that betrayed an intent to interrupt or interfere with freedom of movement. The exclusionary rule applied to egregious police conduct, according to the dissent, despite what it termed the Court's "logic-chopping analysis" and "literal-minded[ness]." The majority's concern with the containment of criminal activity, Justice Stevens charged, posed a threat to values that are "fundamental and enduring."[25] These values lay within the protective overlay of the Fourth Amendment and the deterrent effects, if any, conveyed by the exclusionary rule as its essential concomitant.

In the event of a warrantless arrest, it is accepted lore that the Fourth Amendment requires a probable cause determination completed without undue delay or, as the Court expressed it in 1975,[26] "either before or promptly after arrest." What constitutes a prompt conclusory proceeding has remained uncertain whether judged by reference to the Fourth Amendment or traditional common-law guarantees. The Court, in *County of Riverside v. McLaughlin*,[27] sought to establish workable guidelines for the states to follow in providing a flexible framework, striking an appropriate balance between the competing law enforcement needs and the individual's liberty interests, and affording deference to considerations of federalism. The result was a formula permitting judicial determinations of probable cause within 48 hours of arrest as indicative of compliance with the promptness requirement. Such a determination, allowing a combination of a probable cause determination with arraignment procedures, would be "immune from systemic challenges." Toward this end, Justice O'Connor wrote for the majority, "accommodation can take place without running afoul of the Fourth Amendment."[28]

To the dissenters, led by Justice Marshall, a probable cause hearing had to be provided immediately following completion of administrative procedures incident to arrest. Justice Scalia, dissenting separately, went further in extending protection to the "presumptively innocent" detainee. He found it to be an "unreasonable" seizure within the strictures of the Fourth Amendment for a delay in the determination of probable cause to reach beyond 24 hours after the arrest. Justice Scalia referred to the "image" of a system of justice that, in his view, had "lost its ancient sense of priority" grounded not only in the Bill of Rights but in venerable doctrines of the common law. It was Justice Scalia's emphasis on the "original intent" of the Framers, central to his exposition of the Fourth Amendment's requirements, that seemed to dissuade Justice Marshall, joined by Justices Blackmun and Stevens, from subscribing to Scalia's insistence upon a rigorous promptness proviso. Doubtless fears of reinforcing expansive arguments in favor of a strict reliance upon the constitutional text and extolling a "Jurisprudence of Original Intention" were critical in their decision not to become associated with Justice Scalia's forceful discourse.

Apart from decisions revising the criteria governing the several stages of the trial process in criminal cases generally, the most compelling developments were those altering conditions touching upon capital punishment. Questions regarding jury selection in a capital murder case arose in relation to a much-publicized murder by an inmate while out of prison on work detail.[29] Under the circumstances, it was repeatedly asked, how was the accused to be afforded his Sixth Amendment right to an impartial jury and to due process under the Fourteenth Amendment? The majority, speaking through Chief Justice Rehnquist, found no constitutional requirement that "content" questions be put to each of the jurors concerning publicity. Justice Marshall, dissenting with Justices Blackmun and Stevens, took the majority to task for sanctioning the trial court's elicitation of little more than a "simple profession of openmindedness." Acceptance of such a minimal mode of judgment, Marshall charged, had converted a critical constitutional guarantee into a "hollow formality."[30]

Other issues affecting capital punishment related to the status of the accused. Among the factors to be considered at the penalty phase of a trial for capital murder, the mental retardation of the accused ranked high among the elements that might be taken to be mitigating. Was there a categorical prohibition against the execution of persons lacking the ability to understand the wrongfulness of the acts committed? Did this derive from the Eighth Amendment's cruel and unusual punishment clause or from a compelling societal consensus? Justice O'Connor, who wrote for a doctrinally fragmented Court in *Penry v. Lynaugh*,[31] declined to interpose the Eighth Amendment as a controlling barrier to execution of the mentally retarded; nor did she find a national consensus against execution although she indicated that evolving standards might one day emerge and provide such a sense of public opinion. Despite these conclusions, Justice O'Connor's opinion was a far-reaching one, exploring an array of competing arguments regarding the punishment of mentally retarded offenders. She opted for individualized determinations concerning imposition of the death penalty and concluded that execution was not contrary to the Eighth Amendment's proportionality requirement.

Among the separate opinions, the conflicting views of the Justices came through in time-honored fashion though hardly as a basis for guiding precedents lucidly serving judges, juries, and the legal community generally. Justice Brennan, joined by Justice Marshall, would have outlawed execution of the mentally retarded because of their lack of a full degree of responsibility for their crimes.[32] Justice Stevens, joined by Justice Blackmun, agreed that Justice O'Connor's statement of the arguments had been "fairly" stated, but he would have reached the opposite conclusion, a holding of unconstitutionality, by reference to them.[33] Justice Scalia, with Chief Justice Rehnquist and Justices White and Kennedy, expressed approval of Justice O'Connor's findings, permitting execution of the mentally retarded, but he condemned any recourse to proportionality theory in resolving Eighth Amendment issues.[34]

To like effect, a divided Court, limited in part to no more than a plurality opinion, rejected a plea that the Eighth Amendment's ban on cruel and unusual punishment prohibited the execution of persons 16 or 17 years of age. Justice Scalia, writing in *Stanford v. Kentucky*,[35] once again rejected the relevance of proportionality analysis. Instead, he argued that such punishment was neither forbidden as cruel and unusual at the time of the Bill of Rights' adoption nor violative of contemporary standards reflected in state laws or jury determinations. Justice Scalia accepted socioscientific or ethicoscientific polls and evidence to the contrary as suitable for the molding of the views of the citizenry but not for the judiciary that, in any event, is not privileged to substitute its "informed judgment" for constitutional language.

Justice O'Connor, concurring in *Stanford*, rejected Justice Scalia's refusal to apply proportionality analysis to Eighth Amendment jurisprudence. She left open the possibility that a national consensus might be reached concerning the execution of teenaged murderers.[36] As expected, Justice Brennan, joined by Justices Marshall, Blackmun, and Stevens, condemned without reservation the execution of juveniles as contrary to the Eighth Amendment. A minimum age of 18 was said to be required before executions could proceed when all relevant factors were taken into account. Like Justice O'Connor, Justice Brennan embraced proportionality theory but, in this instance, to support a finding that imposition of the death penalty was unjustified when applied to young offenders.[37]

If the status decisions proved to be somewhat ambiguous in terms of their long-term effects, a case decided in the early summer of 1991 caused considerable turmoil when measured against the corpus of capital punishment jurisprudence but, more significantly, when weighed against traditional values associated with the doctrine of stare decisis. The Court, speaking through Chief Justice Rehnquist in *Payne v. Tennessee*,[38] overruled two precedents of recent date, one from 1987[39] and the other announced two years later.[40] The issue lay in the assumed Eighth Amendment ban on the presentation and consideration of victim impact evidence by a capital sentencing jury. Such a rule, it was previously averred, was predicated on a presumed lack of relevance to the defendant's "blameworthiness." If the defendant was to be treated as a "uniquely individual" person, neither the harm caused the victim nor the victim's family could be posited at the sentencing phase of a murder trial.[41]

To the contrary, Chief Justice Rehnquest held in *Payne*, the state had a legitimate interest in counteracting mitigating evidence introduced on the defendant's behalf. The victim's uniqueness presumably was as important as that of his killer. Should the victim impact evidence be so "unduly prejudicial" as to threaten the trial's fundamental fairness, a resort to Fourteenth Amendment due process provided an ultimate means of redress. While the majority conceded the "preferred course" of adhering to established precedents, stare decisis was held not to be an "inexorable command," especially in constitutional cases. Unworkable or poorly reasoned decisions, Rehnquist argued, fell outside the pale of cases militating in favor of a strict reliance on precedents per se.[42]

The intensity of the debate over the doctrine of stare decisis—its applicability, its desirability, and its propriety, particularly in regard to recently established precedents—attained new heights in the area of the criminal law. That the Court was determined to reverse course dramatically, even at the expense of newly created case law, bespeaks a campaign marked by exceptional fervor and profuse exercises in result orientation toward the achievement of what the majority apparently considered a long overdue reformulation of standards. Judicial activism, it appears, need not always be associated with an overweening liberalism. To a greater extent than is usually evident in periodic policy transformations, the prevailing majority was not content merely to erode precedents or to incorporate artful alterations, principally at the periphery. It is noteworthy that the body of law selected for particular scrutiny was the criminal law. Nor is it inaccurate to surmise that this remarkable cycle of change occurred in consonance with and perhaps in response to a public anti-crime animus that had been developing for more than a decade.

That the Court's decision in *Payne* reflects elements of politicization appears from a number of indicators peculiar to the litigation as well as other extrinsic "signals." In mid-February 1991, the Court expedited consideration of the case, establishing a schedule for prompt filings and for oral argument. Additionally, the parties were specifically requested to brief and to argue whether the 1987 and 1989 precedents prescribing the inadmissibility of victim impact evidence should be overruled. At the time, Justice Stevens, joined by Justices Marshall and Blackmun, termed the Court's unusual request and its "reaching out" for an expeditious review "both unwise and unnecessary."[43] A further special note lay in the appearance of the Attorney General, who argued for the Government as amicus curiae, thus lending substantial support to the state's cause. The Attorney General rarely appears as amicus. In the relatively few cases in which the Government intervenes when it is not a party of record, it is the Solicitor General who presents any briefs and argument on behalf of the United States.

Has the Court embarked upon a purposeful campaign to rewrite the criminal law of the states? Is this an effort intended, at least in some measure, to meet the demands of a citizenry bent upon redressing the balance in a society looked upon as increasingly crime-ridden, abetted by an unduly indulgent and pro-defendant judiciary? Surely a majority would have little difficulty in treating sternly the infliction of capital punishment where any "opposition constituency," if one could be termed such, would not be a formidable one. If public opinion looms as an unwritten factor in judicial decision making, there is no comparability between such sensitive questions as those related to liberty and privacy interests, particularly as these are manifested in the abortion controversy, and any issue related to the criminal law, much less the fate of convicted murderers.

It may be unseemly, as Justice Stevens noted in his dissent in *Payne*, for a court to take on the role of a legislature in assessing the political appeal of arguments advanced.[44] The "victim rights" movement ought not to be considered in the resolution of constitutional questions by the nation's highest court. Instead, as Justice Stevens prophesied, it may be a "sad day for a great institution."[45] Justice Marshall was even more emphatic in assailing the majority's endeavor as one that would "squander the authority and the legitimacy" of the Court as a "protector of the powerless."[46] Whether, in fact, there has been a failure to differentiate between legislative determinations and judicial sentencing remains an open question though one that ought not to be raised at all when the mandate of the Eighth Amendment is at stake.

Apart from capital punishment sentencing cases, the future of defendant rights appears to be bleak but not necessarily as disheartening as the dissenters in *Payne* appear to have projected. That Warren Court precedents may well survive as lusterless shells of a past era seems likely, but a downgrading of these precedents had been predictable for more than two decades. The Fourth Amendment doubtless will continue to be given less credibility as a viable constitutional safeguard, and the controversial exclusionary rule may decline still further if it is not wholly set aside. Yet it is not at all clear that what Justice Stevens in *Payne* referred to as the "trivialization" of the doctrine of stare decisis will take on additional momentum. The Court, a conservative institution since its inception two centuries ago, may not follow a precipitous course marked by a cavalier abandonment of precedents. To do so in the criminal justice area, even on a presumed wave of favorable public opinion, bodes ill for the future and threatens pronouncements far more significant and measurably more closely linked to the predilections of the prevailing majority.

NOTES

1. 384 U.S. 436 (1966).
2. 367 U.S. 643 (1961).
3. The rule was first introduced as a requirement in the federal courts in Weeks v. United States, 232 U.S. 383 (1914).
4. *See* Bivens v. Six Unknown Named Agents, 403 U.S. 388 (1971).
5. United States v. Leon, 468 U.S. 897 (1984).
6. *See e.g.*, Gideon v. Wainwright, 372 U.S. 335 (1963); Malloy v. Hogan, 378 U.S. 1 (1964); Murphy v. Waterfront Comm., 378 U.S. 52 (1964); Griffin v. California, 380 U.S. 609 (1965).
7. See Yale Kamisar, *The "Police Practice" Phases of the Criminal Process and the Three Phases of the Burger Court, in* THE BURGER YEARS (Herman Schwartz, ed., 1989).
8. Rogers v. Richmond, 365 U.S. 534 (1961).
9. Payne v. Arkansas, 356 U.S. 560 (1958).
10. 113 L. Ed. 2d 302 (1991).
11. *Id.* at 331.
12. *Id.* at 318.
13. *Id.* at 320–21.
14. 113 L. Ed. 2d 517 (1991).
15. *Id.* at 541.
16. *Id.* at 545–46.
17. *Id.* at 559.
18. A further narrowing of access to habeas corpus review occurred in *Coleman v. Thompson*, 115 L. Ed 2d 640 (1991), when the Court, through Justice O'Connor, precluded presentation of the accused's claims, predicated on independent and adequate state grounds and founded in "concerns of comity and federalism." Justice Blackmun, dissenting with Justices Marshall and Stevens, termed the majority's commentary a "Byzantine morass of arbitrary, unnecessary, and unjustifiable impediments to the vindication of federal rights." *Id.* at 675.
19. 115 L. Ed. 2d 389 (1991).
20. *Id.* at 408.

21. 114 L. Ed. 2d 619 (1991).
22. *Id.* at 648. For measurement of a suspect's consent to a search, *see* Florida v. Jimeno, 114 L. Ed. 2d 297 (1991).
23. *See, e.g.*, Katz v. United States, 389 U.S. 347 (1967) and Terry v. Ohio, 392 U.S. 1 (1968).
24. 113 L. Ed. 2d 690 (1991).
25. *Id.* at 711.
26. Gerstein v. Pugh, 420 U.S. 103, 125 (1975).
27. 114 L. Ed. 2d 49 (1991).
28. *Id.* at 64.
29. Mu'Min v. Virginia, 114 L. Ed. 2d 493 (1991).
30. *Id.* at 511.
31. 492 U.S. 302 (1989).
32. *Id.* at 341.
33. *Id.* at 349–50.
34. *Id.* at 351–60.
35. 492 U.S. 361 (1989).
36. *Id.* at 381–82.
37. *Id.* at 383–405.
38. 115 L. Ed. 2d 720 (1991).
39. Booth v. Maryland, 482 U.S. 496 (1987).
40. South Carolina v. Gathers, 490 U.S. 805 (1989).
41. 482 U.S. at 502, 504.
42. 115 L. Ed. 2d at 737.
43. *See* 112 L. Ed. 2d 1032–33 (1991).
44. 115 L. Ed. 2d at 758–60.
45. *Id.* at 763.
46. *Id.* at 756.

8

Concluding Observations:
Glimpses of the Road Ahead

The ebb and flow of judicial rulings, consequential when viewed in the aggregate, offer clues to the future course of the Rehnquist Court and to the nature of decision making that may reasonably be expected to control. Much depends on the vicissitudes of the appointing process as the Court continues to move through the final decade of the twentieth century into the opening years of a new millenium. If, in fact, the Rehnquist era previously had begun to take on a recognizable identity, notions of a coherent majority, veering to the far Right of the political spectrum, proved to be premature and unreliable. Instead, a moderately directed conservative coalition has emerged, pledged to no abiding ideological agenda that can be regarded as overweening. A measure of temperance has returned to a Court that, for the past half-decade, had seemed determined to effectuate a counterrevolution of major proportions. Whether or not the new working majority will remain secure in the light of pressures of superannuation, general personnel instability, and uncertain executive-legislative politics continues to be problematic in its reach and ultimate results.

Like the Burger Court that preceded it, the Rehnquist Court is unlikely to move decisively to depart from pragmatic moorings unless prevailing coalitions change dramatically.[1] A marked reversal of course no longer appears to be probable in view of the centrist principles announced during the 1991 term, especially its culminating phase that marked the early summer of 1992. Doubtless alliances will continue to shift, as they have over the years, but any outcroppings of "superconservatism" may well be noticeably rare and, in effect, restrained within the bounds of institutional propriety. It is questionable whether a proliferation of aberrant retreats from a new-found, mid-spectrum consensus will occur if demythologizing tendencies are to be held in check and reserves of public trust are not to be needlessly sacrificed. The erratic development of American constitutional law predictably will continue to dominate; its ephemeral and often mundane characteristics will remain notably in evidence; and the long-term responsiveness of the Court to American public opinion will still provide the rudiments of a judicial context that has always revealed a measure of accountability by an anti-majoritarian body when and if the electorate is unequivocally determined to have its way.

To the surprise of many and the consternation of some, an unexpected community of interest seems to have developed, within a pivotal cadre consisting of Justices Kennedy, O'Connor, and Souter, that may control the outcome of critical decisions. Should this coalition remain essentially undisturbed, much of the corrosive effect of the Rehnquist Court's "hard core," represented by the Chief Justice joined by Justices Scalia and Thomas, may be neutralized and eventually set to naught. If it is important to examine possible reasons for the formation of this coalition and the elements that bind it together, it is equally intriguing to weigh the longevity of a group whose members were appointed by presidents bent on achieving political objectives that lay outside the usual purview of the judiciary, if not of a pluralist society traditionally linked to diverse values and plans.

Amidst hints that a new coalition was building in a number of areas,[2] the Court went on to reaffirm its adherence to *Roe v. Wade*[3] as a "simple limitation beyond which a state law is unenforceable" and as a precedent that does not represent a "mere survivor of obsolete constitutional thinking."[4] More important, as a testament of constitutional faith, the trio of Justices described at length a basic credo that avowed the need to weigh carefully the force of the doctrine of stare decisis in the disposition of cases and to take scrupulously into account the Court's public image as an ultimate and respected expositor of the law. Justice Blackmun, the author of the 1973 abortion rights decision, paid tribute to his colleagues' unusual joint opinion as an "act of personal courage and constitutional principle." Yet, while Blackmun's characterization was plainly warranted, the opinion disclosed far more—exceptional discourse in relation to topical motifs not often touched upon in the annals of the Court.

Apart from the abortion issue as such, the opinion cited the school desegregation case[5] and *Roe v. Wade* as seminal decisions that, as the three Justices put it, called the "contending sides of a national controversy to end their national division by accepting a common mandate in the Constitution."[6] The Court took liberty and personal autonomy as its predicate. But it also moved with considerable vigor to reject any easy overruling of a precedent if the central holding would not only reach an unjustifiable result but would impair the Court's capacity to function in appropriate, time-honored fashion. The prevailing faction rejected any constitutional holding that would jeopardize the nation's commitment to the rule of law and cast doubt upon the Court's legitimacy.[7] In a remarkable sideswipe directed against persistent pressures from the executive branch and from a vocal minority of anti-abortion advocates, the newly formed bloc asserted its aversion to surrender to political demands or to "overrule under fire." Public acceptance of the Court's pronouncements, it was alleged, must be grounded in principle "not as compromises with social and political pressures" whatever their source.[8]

The mood of the centrist coalition, surely not to be dismissed as a passing or trifling anomaly, has been portrayed by Kenneth Starr, the former Bush Administration's Solicitor General, as a significant alteration of course much in the spirit of former Justice Lewis F. Powell's commentaries and oft-stated, mid-spectrum convictions.

There is a disinclination, if not a decided antipathy, to enter upon the reconsideration of accepted doctrines merely at the behest of presidential urgings conveyed by the Solicitor General. In part, revulsion against such promptings may have accounted for the unusual display of adherence to traditional principles of judicial review in the abortion rights case. Whether this is no more than a plea for the respect due the doctrine of stare decisis or a broader rejection of precipitous shifts brought on by politically impelled forces remains open to contention and further debate. The fervor of the joint opinion suggests that the latter sentiment will prevail unless contrary personnel actions militate against the conclusions reached.

That members of the Court have been troubled by the past Administration's repeated prodding is evident from scattered references in the opinions. A clash that attracted special attention occurred in the spring of 1992 when, in a case raising questions of prosecutorial misconduct on the part of the Government,[9] a majority upheld the Justice Department's claims. Justice Stevens, in dissent, charged that the Court's treatment of the issues, initially its willingness to proceed in the matter, might be taken to "favor" the Government over the ordinary litigant, thereby compromising the obligation to administer justice impartially. In the abortion rights case subsequently decided, the joint opinion referred disparagingly to the Government's persistent efforts to have the Court overrule *Roe v. Wade* in five other cases during the past decade.[10]

It need hardly be stressed that most cases do not fall within highly sensitive categories that occasion affective responses. In the final days of the Court's 1991–92 term, a cluster of decisions pointed to recurrent themes that arise despite routine changes in focus and subject matter coverage. Several recent Commerce Clause questions, for example, have related to refuse disposal and local attempts to bar the receipt of solid waste products and hazardous materials generated out-of-state.[11] The Court's characterization of these measures as discriminatory and protectionist in nature is not notably new or different from previous controversies though the objects of "negative" or "dormant" Commerce Clause review are dissimilar. To like effect are cases touching upon the reach of state taxation, a physical-presence nexus linked to due process, the Commerce Clause, and statutory preemption.[12] In all of these areas, each closely associated with consideration of significant aspects of American federalism, major doctrinal alterations are not likely to be introduced.

It should also be noted that the Rehnquist Court, even more than its predecessor, does not impart a sense of exclusivity as the final source of judgment or expository wisdom in the disposition of all manner of disputed or highly contentious questions besetting American society. The Court, in effect, has held that state appellate courts are better equipped to deal with such personal autonomy issues as the right-to-die[13] and that, in many respects, state-created precedents ought to be followed as more exactingly relevant than the sparse federal decisional law on the subect. More broadly stated, the Justices have consciously deferred to state courts, premising their findings on independent and adequate state grounds, in a contemporary revival of state constitutional law hitherto unknown.[14] It is demonstrably apparent that liberty and privacy interests will not advance substantially in a federal forum controlled by the current array of Justices. Instead, state constitutional principles are likely to remain the principal predicates of judicial review in this as in other areas.

Less often looked upon as impressive, but surely not to be wholly disregarded, is congressional attention to constitutional questions at relevant stages of the legislative process and in the several phases of implementation. If the stress upon original intent and the design of lawmakers is to be more than a vague and meaningless ruse, the historic role of Congress ought not to be discounted as cavalierly as the popular media and many more serious critics often counsel. A Freedom of Choice Act, intended to assure and perhaps to expand the scope of abortion rights, lies within the range of achievable legislative powers by way of the Enforcement Clause of the Fourteenth Amendment and the Commerce Clause. And, if past accomplishment serves as a reminder of future performance, the responsibility of Congress in twice defeating efforts to alter the wording of the First Amendment (prompted by the flag desecration cases)[15] ranks high in reaffirming legislative trustworthiness in safeguarding the Bill of Rights. The participation of the representative branch in defending the integrity of the Constitution ought not to be casually discounted and set aside as without merit. Since the Rehnquist Court has not been an object of widespread acclaim thus far, alternative fora need to be considered and weighed in an assessment of the possible sources of creative constitutional activism.

NOTES

1. For reviews of the Burger years, *see* VINCENT BLASI, ed., THE BURGER COURT: THE COUNTER-REVOLUTION THAT WASN'T (1983) and CHARLES M. LAMB AND STEPHEN C. HALPERN, eds., THE BURGER COURT: POLITICAL AND JUDICIAL PROFILES (1991). Earlier eras, in their sweep and effect, are treated in ROBERT G. MCCLOSKEY, THE AMERICAN SUPREME COURT (1960) and BENJAMIN F. WRIGHT, THE GROWTH OF AMERICAN CONSTITUTIONAL LAW (1942).

2. *See, e.g.*, Lee v. Weisman, 120 L. Ed. 2d 467 (1992), the public school graduation prayer case and International Society for Krishna Consciousness v. Lee, 120 L. Ed. 2d 541 (1992), particularly the literature distribution section.

3. 410 U.S. 113 (1973).

4. Planned Parenthood of Southeastern Pa. v. Casey, 120 L. Ed. 2d 674, 701 (1992).

5. Brown v. Board of Education, 347 U.S. 483 (1954).

6. 120 L. Ed. 2d at 708.

7. *Id.* at 706–9.

8. *Id.*

9. United States v. Williams, 118 L. Ed. 2d 352 (1992).

10. 120 L. Ed. 2d at 693.

11. Chemical Waste Management v. Hunt, 119 L. Ed. 2d 121 (1992); Fort Gratiot Sanitary Landfill v. Michigan Dept. of Natural Resources, 119 L. Ed. 2d 139 (1992).

12. Quill Corp. v. North Dakota, 119 L. Ed. 2d 91 (1992); Morales v. Trans World Airlines, 119 L .Ed. 2d 157 (1992).

13. Cruzan v. Director, Missouri Dept. of Public Health, 497 U.S. 261 (1990).

14. *See* Stanley H. Friedelbaum, *Judicial Federalism: Current Trends and Long-Term Prospects*, 19 FLA. ST. U. L. R. 1053–88 (1992).

15. Texas v. Johnson, 491 U.S. 397 (1989); United States v. Eichman, 496 U.S. 310 (1990).

Selected Bibliography

Ackerman, Bruce A. "Beyond *Carolene Products.*" *Harvard Law Review* 98 (1985): 713–46.

Advisory Commission on Intergovernmental Relations. "The Federal Courts: Intergovernmental Umpires or Regulators?" *Intergovernmental Perspective* 18 (Fall 1992): 12–15.

_____. "Federalism and Constitutional Rights." *Intergovernmental Perspective* 17 (Fall 1991): 5–48.

_____. *Regulatory Federalism: Policy, Process, Impact and Reform.* Washington: The Commission, 1984.

Berger, Raoul. "New Theories of 'Interpretation': The Activist Flight From the Constitution." *Ohio State Law Journal* 47 (1986): 1–45.

Beschle, Donald L. "Autonomous Decisionmaking and Social Choice: Examining the 'Right to Die.' " *Kentucky Law Journal* 77 (1989): 319–67.

Bork, Robert H. *The Tempting of America: The Political Seduction of the Law.* New York: The Free Press, 1989.

Coenen, Dan T. "Untangling the Market Participant Exemption to the Dormant Commerce Clause." *Michigan Law Review* 88 (1989): 395–488.

Davis, Sue. "Federalism and Property Rights: An Examination of Justice Rehnquist's Legal Positivism." *Western Political Quarterly* 39 (1986): 250–64.

_____. *Justice Rehnquist and the Constitution.* Princeton, N.J.: Princeton University Press, 1989.

152 • SELECTED BIBLIOGRAPHY

_____. "Justice William H. Rehnquist: Right-Wing Ideologue or Majoritarian Democrat?" In *The Burger Court: Political and Judicial Profiles*, edited by Charles M. Lamb & Stephen C. Halpern, 315–42. Urbana & Chicago: University of Illinois Press, 1991.

_____. "Power on the Court: Chief Justice Rehnquist's Opinion Assignments." *Judicature* 74 (1990): 66–72.

Detlefsen, Robert R. *Civil Rights Under Reagan*. San Francisco: Institute for Contemporary Studies, 1991.

Dorf, Michael C. "Captain of the Court?" *Rutgers Magazine* 71, No. 4 (1992): 12–13.

Farber, Daniel A. "Free Speech Without Romance: Public Choice and the First Amendment." *Harvard Law Review* 105 (1991): 554–83.

Farber, Daniel A. and Nowak, John E. "The Misleading Nature of Public Forum Analysis: Content and Context in First Amendment Adjudication." *Virginia Law Review* 70 (1984): 1219–66.

Field, Martha A. "*Garcia v. San Antonio Metropolitan Transit Authority*: The Demise of a Misguided Doctrine." *Harvard Law Review* 99 (1985): 84–118.

Fried, Charles. "*Metro Broadcasting, Inc. v. FCC*: Two Concepts of Equality." *Harvard Law Review* 104 (1990): 107–25.

Friedelbaum, Stanley H. *Contemporary Constitutional Law: Case Studies in the Judicial Process*. Boston: Houghton Mifflin, 1972.

_____. "Deference in Disarray: Conflict and Vacillation in the Burger Court." *Dickinson Law Review* 91 (1986): 187–212.

_____. "Judicial Federalism: Current Trends and Long-Term Prospects." *Florida State University Law Review* 19 (1992): 1053–88.

_____. "Reactive Responses: The Complementary Role of Federal and State Courts." *Publius: The Journal of Federalism* 17 (Winter, 1987): 33–50.

Hafen, Bruce C. "*Hazelwood School District* and the Role of First Amendment Institutions." *1988 Duke Law Journal*: 685–705.

Hershkoff, Helen and Cohen, Adam S. "Begging to Differ: The First Amendment and the Right to Beg." *Harvard Law Review* 104 (1991): 896–916.

Hovenkamp, Herbert. "The Political Economy of Substantive Due Process." *Stanford Law Review* 40 (1988): 379–447.

Howard, A. E. Dick. "*Garcia* and the Values of Federalism: On the Need for a Recurrence to Fundamental Principles." *University of Georgia Law Review* 19 (1985): 789–97.

Kassop, Nancy. "From Arguments to Supreme Court Opinions in *Planned Parenthood v. Casey*." *PS: Political Science & Politics* 26 (1993): 53–58.

Kushner, James A. "Substantive Equal Protection: The Rehnquist Court and the Fourth Tier of Judicial Review." *Missouri Law Review* 53 (1988): 423–63.

McCann, Michael W. and Houseman, Gerald L., eds. *Judging the Constitution: Critical Essays on Judicial Lawmaking*. Boston: Scott, Foresman, 1989.

Maroney, Thomas J. "*Bowers v. Hardwick*: A Case Study in Federalism, Legal Procedure, and Constitutional Interpretation." *Syracuse Law Review* 38 (1987): 1223–50.

Mayton, William T. "Seditious Libel and the Lost Guarantee of a Freedom of Expression." *Columbia Law Review* 84 (1984): 91–142.

Melone, Albert P. "Revisiting the the Freshman Effect Hypothesis: The First Two Terms of Justice Anthony Kennedy." *Judicature* 74 (1990): 6–13.

Michaelman, Frank. "Saving Old Glory: On Constitutional Iconography." *Stanford Law Review* 42 (1990): 1337–64.

Note. "The Battle Between Mother and Fetus: Fetal Protection Policies in the Context of Employment Discrimination." *Hamline Law Review* 14 (1991): 403–26.

_____. "Of Burning Crosses and Chilled Expression: Minnesota and the Eighth Circuit Moderate First Amendment Mandates in 'Hate Speech' Prosecutions." *Hamline Law Review* 15 (1991): 167–93.

_____. "Developments in the Law—Medical Technology and the Law." *Harvard Law Review* 103 (1990): 1519–1676.

_____. "State Power and Discrimination by Private Clubs: First Amendment Protection for Nonexpressive Associations." *Harvard Law Review* 104 (1991): 1835–56.

O'Connor, Karen. "The Effects of the Thomas Nomination on the Supreme Court." *PS: Political Science & Politics* 25 (1992): 492–5.

Ogletree, Charles J., Jr. "*Arizona v. Fulminante*: The Harm of Applying Harmless Error to Coerced Confessions." *Harvard Law Review* 105 (1991): 152–75.

Pacelle, Richard L., Jr. *The Transformation of the Supreme Court's Agenda: From the New Deal to the Reagan Administration.* Boulder: Westview Press, 1991.

Rapaczynski, Andrzej. "From Sovereignty to Process: The Jurisprudence of Federalism after *Garcia*." *1985 Supreme Court Review* 341–419.

Regan, Donald H. "The Supreme Court and State Protectionism: Making Sense of the Dormant Commerce Clause." *Michigan Law Review* 84 (1986): 1091–1287.

Rehnquist, William H. "All Discord, Harmony Not Understood: The Performance of the Supreme Court of the United States." *Arizona Law Review* 22 (1980): 976–86.

_____. *The Supreme Court: How It Was, How It Is.* New York: William Morrow, 1987.

Rhode, Deborah. *Justice and Gender: Sex Discrimination and the Law.* Cambridge: Harvard University Press, 1989.

Rhoden, Nancy K. "Litigating Life and Death." *Harvard Law Review* 102 (1988): 375–94.

Rosenfeld, Michael. *Affirmative Action and Justice: A Philosophical and Constitutional Inquiry.* New Haven: Yale University Press, 1991.

Rubin, Thea F. and Melone, Albert P. "Justice Antonin Scalia: A First Year Freshman Effect?" *Judicature* 72 (1988): 98–102.

Samar, Vincent J. *The Right to Privacy: Gays, Lesbians, and the Constitution.* Philadelphia: Temple University Press, 1991.

Savage, David G. *Turning Right: The Making of the Rehnquist Supreme Court.* New York: Wiley, 1992.

Schwartz, Bernard. "*National League of Cities* Again: R.I.P. or a Ghost that Still Walks." *Fordham University Law Review* 54 (1985): 141–66.

———. *The New Right and the Constitution: Turning Back the Legal Clock.* Boston: Northeastern University Press, 1990.

Schwartz, Herman. "The 1986 and 1987 Affirmative Action Cases: It's All Over But the Shouting." *Michigan Law Review* 86 (1987): 524–76.

Segal, Jeffrey A. and Spaeth, Harold J. "Rehnquist Court Disposition of Lower Court Decisions: Affirmation Not Reversal." *Judicature* 74 (1990): 84–88.

Simsom, Gary J. "The Establishment Clause in the Supreme Court: Rethinking the Court's Approach." *Cornell Law Review* 72 (1987): 905–35.

Sinclair, Barbara. "Senate Process, Congressional Politics, and the Thomas Nomination." *PS: Political Science & Politics* 25 (1992): 477–80.

Smith, C. Calvin. "The Civil Rights Legacy of Ronald Reagan." *Western Journal of Black Studies* 14 (1990): 102–14.

Smith, Steven D. "Symbols, Perceptions, and Doctrinal Illusions: Establishment, Neutrality, and the 'No Endorsement' Test." *Michigan Law Review* 86 (1987): 266–332.

Sterk, Stewart E. "The Continuity of Legislatures: Of Contracts and the Contracts Clause." *Columbia Law Review* 88 (1988): 647–722.

Stern, Nat. "State Action, Establishment Clause, and Defamation: Blueprints for Civil Liberties in the Rehnquist Court." *University of Cincinnati Law Review* 57 (1989): 1175–1242.

Sullivan, Kathleen M. "Unconstitutional Conditions." *Harvard Law Review* 102 (1989): 1413–1506.

Swanson, Wayne R. *The Christ Child Goes to Court.* Philadelphia: Temple University Press, 1990.

Taylor, Stuart. "Rehnquist's Court: Tuning Out the White House." *The New York Times Magazine*, September 11, 1988, pp. 38–41, 94–95, 98.

Tribe, Laurence H. and Dorf, Michael C. *On Reading the Constitution.* Cambridge: Harvard University Press, 1991.

Van Alstyne, William W. "The Second Death of Federalism." *Michigan Law Review* 83 (1985): 1709–33.

Vieira, Norman. "*Hardwick* and the Right of Privacy." *University of Chicago Law Review* 55 (1988): 1181–91.

Walker, Samuel. *In Defense of American Liberties—A History of the ACLU.* New York: Oxford University Press, 1990.

Wellington, Harry H. *Interpreting the Constitution: The Supreme Court and the Process of Adjudication.* New Haven: Yale University Press, 1990.

Wenz, Peter S. *Abortion Rights as Religious Freedom*. Philadelphia: Temple University Press, 1992.

Yarbrough, Tinsley E., ed. *The Reagan Administration and Human Rights*. New York: Praeger, 1985.

Table of Cases

Index

status of commercial speech as protected expression, 61–62, 63–64; and tax exemption for religious periodicals, 103–4

Blackstone, Sir William, and press freedom, 73

Blue Laws. *See* Sunday Closing Laws

Brennan, Justice William: and charitable solicitation, 55–56; and church's claim for Civil Rights Act exemption, 102; and "constitutionalization" of the law of libel, 74–75; and doubts over endorsement test and religious pluralism, 99; and execution of minors and the mentally retarded, 138–39; and expressive activities on postal sidewalks, 54–55; and federal-state powers, 6, 8; and flag-burning as expressive freedom, 58–60; and intergovernmental tax immunities, 14; and liberty interests affected by state inaction, 36; and municipal zoning to contain "adult theatres," 81; and obscenity tests, 79–80; and picketing near private homes, 54; and press freedom in public schools, 88; and public employee rights, 48; and right-to-die debate, 40; and secondary effects standard, 81; and sources of liberty interests, 37; and tax exemption for religious periodicals, 103; and unemployment benefits for Sabbatarians, 105

Burger, Chief Justice Warren: and articulation of *Lemon* tests, 97; and expressive freedom in public schools, 87; and public health regulation of "adult" bookstores, 81

Burger Court: and the criminal law, 129; and tests of obscenity, 81; in a transitional state, 129

Capital punishment: and content questions to jurors, 137; and execution of the mentally retarded, 137–38; and execution of minors, 138–39; and proportionality theory, 138–39; and status of the accused, 137–38; and victim impact evidence, 139–40

Centrist coalition: and future course of Rehnquist Court, 146–48; and joint opinion in support of abortion rights, 34

Charitable solicitation, and the First Amendment, 55–56

Clark, Justice Tom C., and state taxation of out-of-state enterprises, 16

Coerced confessions, and due process, 129–31

Commerce Clause: and *Rewis-Bass* guidelines, 5–6; as source of national power, 2

Commercial speech: and diluted First Amendment rights, 63–64; and First Amendment guarantees, 61–64; and out-of-state abortion advertisements, 61

Comstock, Anthony, 79

Contempt power, and out-of-court comment, 85

Criminal law: aspects of, 127–43; changes in Burger Court, 129; and Fourteenth Amendment's due process clause, 127; and *Miranda* warnings, 127–28; in Warren Court, 128–29

Defamation, law of: and actual malice standard, 74–75; and breach of assured confidentiality, 77–78; and emotional distress as

Green factors, as basis for unitary school system, 117

Habeas corpus petitions: abuse of writ doctrine, 131–33; "cause and prejudice" rule, 132; "deliberate abandonment" standard rejected, 132–33; narrowing of access to, 142 n.18; and questions of federalism, 131–32; and state courts, 131–33; and state exhaustion doctrine, 133

Harlan, Justice John M.: and actual malice standard, 75; and concept of ordered library, 30; and constitutional code for confessions, 128; and Fair Labor Standards Act extension to state and local employees, 4; and flag desecration, 57

Harmless-error standards, and involuntary confessions, 130–31

Homosexual sodomy, and privacy interests, 34–35

Intergovernmental immunities, doctrine of, and tax-exempt interest on municipal bonds, 12–15

Jefferson, Thomas, and wall-of-separation metaphor, 95

Kennedy, Justice Anthony: and ban on out-of-court comment, 86; and "cause and prejudice" rule in habeas corpus cases, 132; and efforts to end judicial supervision of school desegregation, 116–17; and expressive activities on postal sidewalks, 54; and flag-burning as expressive behavior, 59; and misgivings over endorsement test, 99, 102

Lawless, Luke, 85

Lawyer advertising cases, and First Amendment rights, 62

Liberty, due process, and heterosexual relations, 30–31; and historic roots, 27–29; and individual autonomy and familial decision-making, 29–30

McCarthy era, litigation arising from, 46–47

Madison, James, and national-state powers, 1

Marshall, Chief Justice John, and national powers, 2

Marshall, Justice Thurgood: and affirmative action programs, 119; call for institutional disassociation from religious speech and group goals, 102; and content questioning of prospective jurors, 137; and federal-state balance, 6, 7; and Fourth Amendment searches, 134; and habeas corpus relief, 132–33; and probable cause determinations, 136; and public employee rights, 49; and steps to end judicial supervision of school desegregation, 116; and taxability of payments for tasks performed by a religious sect, 104–5; and wage-price controls, 4

Municipal bond interest, taxability of, 12–15

National Minimum Drinking Age Amendment, sustained, 11–12

Neutrality, theory of in Religious Clause cases, 95

Obscenity: *Miller* standards for judgment of, 82; and "secondary effects" analysis, 81; tests of, 79–85

O'Connor, Justice Sandra Day: and
abortion rights, 32–34; and affirmative action programs, 118–
19; and age discrimination
standards and tests, 122; and endorsement corollary in church's
claim for civil rights act exemption, 102; and equal access for
religious groups, 101–2; and
execution of minors and the
mentally retarded, 137–39; and
expressive activities near foreign embassies, 52–53; and expressive activities on postal
sidewalks, 54; and "First
Amendment Free Zone," 51–52;
and formulation of endorsement
test, 98–99; Fourth Amendment
and random bus searches, 134;
and nature of federalism, 10, 12,
14–15; objections to *Lemon*'s
three-pronged test, 97; and perceived excesses of permissible
lawyer advertising, 62; and peyote use, free exercise, and receipt of public benefits, 108;
and picketing near private
homes, 53; and pretextual closing of "adult" bookstores, 82;
and proportionality theory in
capital cases, 137–39; and right-
to-die safeguards, 39; and
sources of liberty interests, 37;
and taxability of payments for
tasks performed by a religious
sect, 105
Ordered liberty, concept of, 30
Original intent, and probable cause
determinations, 136–37
Out-of-court comment, and contempt power, 85

Peck, James H., 85
Powell, Justice Lewis: and equal access for religious meetings, 100–

101; expressive association and
egalitarian interests, 66–67; expressive matters, public and private distinguished, 76; and
nature of federalism, 10; preemption and state anti-corporate
takeover laws, 20–21; and public employee rights, 49
Preemption: and judicial policymaking, 17–18; and pregnancy discrimination act, 18–19; and state
anti-corporate takeover laws,
20–22
Press freedom: extent of in public
schools, 87–88; and fair trial
guarantees, 85–87
Privacy right, and due process liberty, 30
Probable cause determinations, in
Fourth Amendment cases, 136–37
Public employee rights, cases related to, 47–50
Public forum analysis, as a First
Amendment decisional tool, 50–56
Public schools, extent of expressive
freedom in, 87–88

Racial segregation: course of in education, 114–17; de jure and de
facto practices, 115; vestiges of
in state colleges, 124
Racketeer Influenced and Corrupt
Organizations law (RICO), and
obscenity violations, 82
Rehnquist, Chief Justice William
H.: and abortion rights, 32–33;
and ban on out-of-court comment, 86; and charitable solicitation, 56; and content
questioning of prospective jurors, 137; and departures from
stare decisis doctrine, 139–40;
and emotional distress as variant
of defamation, 76–77; and federal-state powers, 14; and flag-

168   •   INDEX

near private homes, 53–54; and preemption issue as related to pregnancy act, 20; and press freedom in public schools, 87–88; and public employee rights, 48; and RICO law applied to obscenity violations, 82; and tax exemption for religious periodicals, 103; and vestiges of segregation in state colleges, 124

Zenger, John Peter, and press freedom, 73

About the Author

STANLEY H. FRIEDELBAUM, Founder and Director of the Burns Center for State Constitutional Studies at Rutgers University in New Brunswick, is the author of *Human Rights in the States: New Directions in Constitutional Policymaking* (Greenwood Press, 1988). He is well known for his writings in state and federal constitutional law.

ISBN 0-313-27990-X

90000>

EAN

9 780313 279904

HARDCOVER BAR CODE